YEHUDI MENUHIN MUSIC GUIDES

ORGAN

YEHUDI MENUHIN MUSIC GUIDES

Organ

Arthur Wills

SCHIRMER BOOKS
A Division of Macmillan, Inc.
NEW YORK

I dedicate this book with love to my wife, Mary, whose invaluable help and encouragement throughout its preparation included the typing of its manuscript in her usual immaculate fashion, and who claims to have learned much from it in the process!

A.W.

Shirmer Books
A Division of Macmillan, Inc.
866 Third Avenue, New York, N.Y. 10022

First American Edition 1985

Library of Congress Catalog Card Number: 84-22180

Printed in Great Britain

printing number (hc.)
1 2 3 4 5 6 7 8 9 10

printing number (pbk.)
1 2 3 4 5 6 7 8 9 10

Library of Congress Cataloging in Publication Data

Wills, Arthur, 1926–
  Organ.
  (Yehudi Menuhin music guides)
  1. Organ—History.   2. Organ music—History and
criticism.   I. Title.   II. Series.
ML550.W39 1985   786.6′2   84-22180
ISBN 0-02-872840-8 (hc.)
ISBN 0-02-872850-5 (pbk.)

Contents

A Note on Stop and Compass Pitches

8′ denotes the length of the longest open pipe of its rank and the sound produced corresponds to the pitch (unison) of the same note on the piano. 4′ and 2′, 16′ and 32′ give the pitch one and two octaves above and below respectively and so on.

Compass pitches are shown as follows:

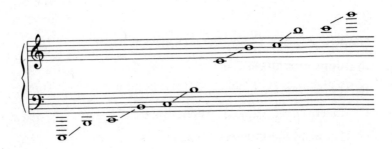

Preface by Yehudi Menuhin

The organ is about as far removed from the voice or the stringed instrument as it is possible to be. Where the latter sustains a sound and modulates it throughout its length, the organ has always seemed to me an instrument of the elements, a superhuman instrument born of wind and rock, of air and shapes. In our churches its sounds represent the disembodied voice of God. Yet it is not only majesty and awe and, by the same token, communal reverence, that this great instrument conveys; its various stops permit of a differentiation of sound register and quality ideally suited to fugal construction. Thus it is in a further sense elemental, for it links the mind of the Creator (or the Universal Mind if you prefer) with the human mind.

The structure of a fugue is not unlike the generating life of a complex molecule. The mind of Johann Sebastian Bach could encompass in its power and penetration every possible commutation and permutation of a given theme, together with appropriate pairing of counter-subject, developments, divertimento periods (*Zwischenspiel* and always the crowning glory of themes expanded, contracted, reversed in both ways (back to front and mirror) as we can see in his 'Art of the Fugue'. This work was conceived as pure music, pure sound structure with no instruments indicated and it seems to me probable that if he ever gave it voice, beyond the sound and the shape in his mind's ear, it must have been on the organ.

Using many manuals, his own feet, other hands to man the stops and other feet to tread the bellows (before the days of electrical or water pumps), he dominates the huge mechanical functions, he is truly a *Deus ex machina*.

The only personal freedom the organist enjoys, and one that requires the greatest discretion, good taste and sense

of inner structure and style is in the very slightest uneven-
ness in the spacing of equal notes, values and phrases.
This one opportunity brings a precious personal commitment to what might otherwise be a boring succession of
even notes. His art in this respect likens that of the harpsi-
chordist, who also handles fixed registers, textures and
volumes.

Above all, unlike the tenor and the violinist, who may
be proverbially mindless so long as they make a beautiful
and moving sound, the organist must be a real musical
mind to do justice to the nature and scope of his
instrument!

In considering the instrument and its player, we come
to its most sublime manifestation – the improvisation of
fugues, preludes and all manner of chorales, etc., which is
the province of the great organist.

Dr Arthur Wills, director of music at Ely Cathedral, is
not just a great organist and, therefore, eminently qualified to write this book but he is one of the greatest experts
in the field of improvisation, having written extensively
on the subject; he has given many recitals and made
numerous recordings. He is also a fine composer. I am
extremely grateful to him for having contributed to this
series and for having written so comprehensively and
entertainingly on this splendid instrument.

Foreword by Stephen Cleobury

When Mozart described the organ as 'the king of instruments' he was referring to something other than the huge
romantic organ of the early twentieth century and the
electronic instruments of today, though a computer could,
no doubt, perform his pieces 'for a mechanical clock' with

accuracy if not good taste. We shall never know what the king of organ composers, the great Kapellmeister of Leipzig, would have thought of the developments in organ-building during the century following his death, but, assuredly, he was closely interested in the art, and his practice of first 'testing the lungs' of an instrument new to him shows that he was not averse to a full sound. Mozart would also have had in mind the splendour of the organ cases that were a notable feature of the magnificent church architecture of the Austria of his day, for then the construction of the case was still closely bound up with the design of the instrument as a whole.

This kingly, majestic ('regal' had better be avoided!) instrument has often made demands on its player that have accorded him a certain importance within the musical profession and, through the Church, within his own local community. Notwithstanding the possible disadvantages of ranging over too wide a field, many organists have displayed great versatility in carrying out many differing tasks assigned to them – solo performance, improvisation and accompaniment, choir-training and conducting, teaching and adjudicating, arranging and composing. Such is the daily round of the English cathedral organist, and there are many musicians now at work in all branches of the profession who have reason to be grateful to this tradition and its guardians for their early training. I shall always value the insights that I gained as a pupil of Dr Wills who, as one of the longest serving cathedral organists of our day, is ideally qualified to write this survey of the organ.

As the reader pursues his course through virtually every facet of the organ, its design, its history, and its music, he will surely find himself sharing Mozart's admiration and enthusiasm for it; let the organist be reminded, however, that the fascination of its mechanism and the attraction of its power must not obscure his main aim, which is to make music.

Introduction

As my interest in the organ is mainly in its music, this book will look at the instrument from the point of view of a musician, rather than from that of an organist or organ-builder.

The instrument's long association with Western Christianity – something that goes far beyond its mere convenience for use in church services – is of profound importance to me, and an understanding of the *philosophy* of the organ and its music will therefore play a larger role than attention to the technical details of organ construction, which are easily obtainable from other sources.

Peter Williams, in his *A New History of the Organ*, has written that 'in the past lies the future of the organ' and considerable space is devoted here to a consideration of the history of the instrument and the consequent implications for its future.

There is a vast literature of music for the organ, the most significant areas being the pre-nineteenth-century periods. The problems arising from the differences between the baroque and romantic approaches are as fully explored as space will allow. The nineteenth century did produce some work of importance, much of which lies behind developments in the twentieth. The implications of the developments of the last hundred years in both organ design and the literature for the music of the future are discussed, keeping in mind that technical considerations in both fields stem from the spiritual and philosophical approach adopted.

An important historical role of the organ has been its use as an adjunct to church services and as accompaniment for choral music. This important function of the instrument has frequently been overlooked or deliberately downgraded by enthusiastic advocates of organ reform movements, although no one thinks that the role of the piano in songs by such composers as Schumann and Wolf diminishes the essential nature of that instrument. In the case of England, the use of the instrument in accompaniment has even – in some cases – begun to overshadow its role as a solo instrument.

This book is also intended for use as a tutor through the study of actual music, rather than through technical exercises. The repertoire to be studied is related to the instrument in its appropriate context and a coherent and logically graded scheme of instruction (see chapter twenty-one) has been suggested.

One of the most fascinating aspects of organ culture has been the survival of the art of improvisation – unique outside the field of jazz. This stems from the time when musicians were expected to be all-rounders – creative as well as performing artists – and also from the ceremonial requirements of church liturgies. Chapters twenty-two and twenty-three outline a scheme of study, requiring disciplined dedication as well as natural flair. It is approached from an historical standpoint and its close relationship to the rest of the book will be obvious.

It will be apparent from my treatment of the idea of the organ as a 'wondrous machine' that there is much more to the study of this instrument than its immediate attraction to the amateur and general public – an impressive sound easily available through the manipulation of ranks of intriguing gadgets. Anyone with a lively interest in the current state of thinking on the development of the organ and its music must not be content with knowledge gained from books, however comprehensive and perceptive. It is necessary to keep up to date by reading periodicals, including past issues. Among the most useful are *Organ Year Book*, *Diapason*, *Organists' Quarterly* and *Journal of the British Institute of Organ Studies*.

One
Wondrous Machines

Wondrous Machine!
To thee the Warbling Lute,
Though us'd to Conquest, must be forced to yield:
With thee unable to dispute,
The Airy Violin,
And Lofty Viol quit the Field;
In vain they tune their speaking Strings
To court the cruel Fair, or praise Victorious Kings,
Whilst all thy consecrated Lays
Are to more noble Uses bent;
And every gratefull Note to Heav'n repays
The Melody it lent.
In vain the Am'rous Flute and soft Guitarr,
Jointly labour to inspire
Wanton Heat and loose Desire;
Whilst thy chast Airs do gently move
Seraphic Flame and Heav'nly Love.
The Fife and all the Harmony of War,
In vain attempt the Passions to alarm,
Which thy commanding Sounds compose and charm.
Let these among themselves contest,
Which can discharge its single Duty best.
Thou summ'st their diff'ring Graces up in One,
And art a Consort of them All within thy self alone.

Nicholas Brady (1659–1726)

The use of the word *machine* in Nicholas Brady's enthusiastic tribute to the organ ('Ode on St Cecilia's Day, 1692')
suggests that, as early as the seventeenth century, the
technological aspect of the instrument was already of
immense appeal to its admirers. This emphasis on the
instrument as an ingenious piece of engineering has frequently deflected its adherents away from its primary
purpose, which is of course the same as any other instrument: to be an appropriate medium for music.

The mechanically simpler instruments, such as the string
family, or the flute, do not possess this fatal temptation,
and artists such as Yehudi Menuhin or James Galway do
not normally expect their audiences to have come primarily to wonder at the instrument rather than the performance it exists to serve. The question 'What is a violin?'
has a fairly simple answer. The instrument has changed
little since the seventeenth century and, even if one men-
tions the viol family and baroque violin, the relationship
between the instruments remains basic and clear: one hand
stops the string in order to produce the required pitch, the
other bow or plucks it in order to set it in vibration and
'speak'.

The same question, asked of the organ, demands a
lengthy and complicated answer. 'A large wind instrument'
is a fairly obvious definition, but this will include – even
within a single country – instruments as diverse as the 7-
stop specification by Handel, for a one-manual organ by
Bridge (1749), to the 102-stop specification by Ralph
Downes for the Royal Festival Hall in London. Despite the
disparity in size both instruments rank as 'large wind
instruments'. However, there is one vital difference between them: the Handel organ would have used a connection between the player's finger and the pipe of a direct,
mechanical kind, essentially no different from such keyboard instruments as the clavichord, harpsichord or piano,
but this intimate relationship of player and instrument is
not present in the RFH scheme. Here the performer sits at
a detached console, at some considerable distance from the

pipes, and air is admitted into the pipe by the activating of an electric switch when the key is depressed.

Clearly, this system puts the organ into a different category from every other instrument, where there is direct physical 'feel' between the player and the production of sound. This 'feel' is of course present whether the instrument is string, wind or percussion, and its absence removes the sensitivity of contact which is taken for granted in these instruments. Nevertheless, the sound in both organs is produced by a vibrating column of air in a pipe, as it is in any orchestral wind instrument.

Small pipe organs were given automatic barrel mechanisms in the eighteenth century. These automatic organs varied in size from Flute Clocks through the Panharmonikon (including percussion) to the Orchestrion. Haydn, Mozart and Beethoven each wrote a small number of works for these instruments, and, a century later, similar mechanisms were applied to the piano.

The nineteenth century saw the invention of the reed organ and harmonium, using free reeds with one resonating chamber. These frequently despised instruments were to be of some importance, notably in Liszt's idea of a combination reed organ and piano (which gives us an insight into his highly individual and innovative style of organ composition) and in the French use of the instrument. Franck's hundred harmonium pieces, and, of more significance, Vierne's *Twenty-four Pieces in Free Style* were important fruits of this relatively humble instrument.

Even the mouth organ found its virtuoso in Larry Adler and the Harmonica Concerto from Vaughan Williams. The secular use of the organ took it into the pleasure garden and the fairground, where, as we shall see, there is good historical precedent for its use.

So far as the pipe organ is concerned, the mid-nineteenth century witnessed radical developments, which, in the name of technological progress, finally shifted the emphasis from the wondrous musical instrument to the ingenious machine. The desire for ever-increasing size and power, for pianistic velocity and orchestral flexibility of tone and dynamics, led to the gradual abandonment of direct mechanical action and eventually to the use of an electrical system which made possible the use of fewer ranks of pipes which could be extended and combined almost without limit. Total enclosure in shuttered boxes put the whole instrument 'under expression'.

These organs found their way into churches but were most frequently used in cinemas. Although originated by an Englishman, Hope-Jones, this type of organ became most associated with the name of Wurlitzer in the USA. This 'unit organ' was already a spurious imitation of a genuine pipe organ of traditional design, and clearly pointed the way to the abandonment of pipes altogether in a complete electronic simulation of organ tone.

It will be seen from this brief résumé that the pre-nineteenth-century pipe organ was gradually falsified in the cause of technological progress, until electronic simulation was seen to be the logical outcome. However, long before this stage was reached, warning voices had been raised, notably by Guilmant in France and Schweitzer in Germany. As a result a tentative return to traditional principles was begun, concentrating first on sound and only later on the construction of mechanical actions.

This only partially answers the question 'What is an organ?' Even when a definition of 'a large wind instrument with mechanical action' is agreed on, before a builder can design and construct an organ for a particular customer, there are many matters still to be considered.

A violin, whether baroque or modern, is more or less the same whether it is found in Italy, France, Germany, Spain or England, but this is far from being the case with the organ. Before 1800, the differences between organs in these countries were so great that the repertoire native to each of them was virtually impossible on the others. The most obvious problem would be in the Pedal department: the German repertoire could not be played on an instrument of any other national school because of differences of compass, character and balance – in England because of the complete absence of a Pedal department. There was, naturally, some cross-fertilization of national ideas, but not on a scale to break down the fundamental differences between them.

Organ-builders frequently complain that organists and consultants either do not know what they want, or ask for conflicting and incompatible styles of instrumental design. The siting of such a large instrument is of course crucial both visually and acoustically. These two aspects of the organ are inextricably linked, since the pipes need to be cased if the tone is to be focused and projected effectively.

If a large instrument of three manuals and pedals and thirty to forty stops is envisaged, then the awkward question of what range of music is to be played on the instrument must be faced. The reeds that suit Couperin will hardly do for Buxtehude and the Celestes needed for Franck will be much too warm and sensual for Howells. The Prinzipal 8′ that is right for Bach will not also double up as the Montre 8′ needed for Vierne.

One solution is to ignore national and particular historic models and build an organ which goes back to such basic principles as lie behind *all* schools of organ-building. But this may well result in an anonymous sound, however beautiful and 'truthful', that reduces all schools, with their varied and fascinating differences of sound, to bland uniformity.

As the early history of the organ will show, the essential characteristic of the basic sound was one of multiple pitches based on the harmonic series. If trying to get maximum variety from a one-manual, 3-stop organ, we might try:

Flute	8′
Principal	4′
Piccolo	2′

This gives a range of colour and dynamic levels of:

forte 8′ 4′ 2′

mezzo-forte 8′ 4′ or 8′ 2′

mezzo-piano   4' either at pitch or an octave lower
piano   8'

So five distinct colours are available from the use of stopping off the individual ranks from the chorus.

For a larger one-manual instrument, we could hardly do better than Handel's scheme of seven stops for the organ now in Great Packington Church:

An Open Diapason – of Metal throughout to be in Front
A Stopt Diapason – the Treble Metal and the Bass Wood
A Principal – of Metal throughout
A Twelfth – of Metal throughout
A Fifteenth – of Metal throughout
A Great Tierce – of Metal throughout
A Flute Stop – such a one as in Mr Freeman's Organ

Handel further specifies: 'One row of keys, whole stops and none in halves.' But if we assume that the Flute would be of 4' pitch, then it would be advantageous to have divided or half-stops for the 8.4.2⅔.2.1⅗. ranks so that these could be used as solo combinations in either treble or bass against 8' and 4' accompanying stops. (Handel's indifference to such textural and colouristic possibilities might warn us against the use of them in his concertos.)

Handel's scheme would enable much of the early German, Italian and English repertoire to be played, but the later German and French repertoire which requires two keyboards for solo and dialogue effects and pedals for solo lines and trio textures would not have been possible. So to this scheme a second keyboard would have to be added, placed either above or below, and both balancing and contrasting with the main chorus. It could consist of:

Flute	8'
Principal	4'
Flute	4'
Flageolet	2'
Larigot	1 ⅓'
Piccolo	1'

The minimum Pedal division to balance this would be:

Bourdon	16'

Organ

Principal	8'
Flute	4'

A reed stop could then be added to each division:

Great Trumpet	8'
Positive Cremona	8'
Pedal Trombone	16'

This of course is just a stop list. As important to the success of the organ would be the skill with which these ranks were scaled and voiced to blend, balance and contrast with each other, in careful relationship to the room in which the organ is sited. Such an instrument could play the entire pre-nineteenth-century repertoire, except for the French *dialogues* which require three manuals for the alternation of the *grand jeu* with a duo of Cromorne and Cornet. The second keyboard could be enclosed in a swell box, but there would be more loss than gain if this was done, as the tonal structure of this instrument is not suitable for nineteenth-century orchestrally inspired music. In any case the swell mechanism cannot produce anything more than a dynamic variation in tone, as opposed to a genuine expressiveness of variation in intensity.

The organ can never be 'expressive' in the personal sense of the violin or the piano – both individualistic instruments of romanticism *par excellence* – but this should be seen as a strength, not as a limitation. The organ can take humanity beyond the expression of human emotions and desires.

The organ design outlined above is clearly not an all-purpose machine. It could play the repertoire already mentioned, together with certain neo-classical pieces such as the Hindemith sonatas, and it could accompany congregational music. Where an entirely new organ is required some limitation is usually necessary on financial grounds and is easily justifiable on purely artistic criteria. But such an instrument cannot begin to be adequate for a really idiosyncratic performance of the many schools of organ music. This problem is bound to remain one of the most controversial aspects of organ design for a very long time.

Two
Organ Actions
and Organ Touch

The best method of connecting the keys with the pipes is a purely mechanical one. On an organ with such a mechanism, phrasing is easiest.

Albert Schweitzer: *The Art of Organ Building and Organ Playing in Germany and France*, 1906

Organ Actions

In any discussion about the respective merits of different types of organ action the words 'light', 'sensitive' and 'responsive' are usually bandied about, often being used without adequate definition. What needs to be made clear from the outset is that tracker actions, rather than the simple on–off electric switch type of mechanism, offer the player the possibility of being able to control the speed of attack of the sound. Without varied attack and release characteristics, notes have a monotonous uniformity which can be likened to human speech without consonants. But some tracker actions are so heavy, sluggish or spongy, and therefore unresponsive, that playing of any kind is impeded, and sensitive playing rendered quite out of the question. Then, certainly, a good electric action seems preferable for any music, and it is clear that for the virtuoso players and composers of the French romantic school in the mid-twentieth century this was the ideal system for their art, the *Etudes* of Jeanne Demessieux being as good an example as any.

19

Key Mechanisms

Despite the strictures of Arnolt Schlick (*c*.1460 – *after* 1527) on the heavy actions of some sixteenth-century builders, it is evident that fully mature key mechanisms had evolved by his time. Two kinds were being developed: a simple action with backfall (see Glossary) was the most common, but a lighter and more responsive action – the *mécanique suspendue* – was also being developed, mainly under the leadership of French builders, and this eliminated the backfall as the pallet was pulled down directly by the key. Some twentieth-century builders, notably Phelps, maintain that this type of action is really effective only on small organs. Nevertheless, the basic principles of these actions would have been known to builders from 1400 onwards.

Coupling

The development of the rollerboard made possible diffuseness of location and an increase in size. As the number of divisions increased the idea of coupling two or more was explored. The concept of coupling suggests adding to the importance of a primary division and this tends to reduce the essential separation and individuality of each keyboard.

In the nineteenth century the main difference of role relationship between the manuals was dynamic rather than in their intrinsic character. This can best be seen in the organs of Cavaillé-Coll: composers such as Franck, Widor and Vierne habitually built their movements around a dynamic structure, passing through the *Récit*, *Positif* and the *Grand Orgue* for a crescendo and contrariwise for a diminuendo. It was probably this technique of 'terraced dynamics' that Schweitzer picked up from his friend Widor and applied to his conception of 'structural' or 'form-rendering' manual changes in the Preludes and Fugues of J. S. Bach. Certainly the use of manual/pedal couplers encouraged the design of less independent Pedal departments. Even the lavish Pedal Organs of Arp Schnitger, such as that at the St Laurens-Kerk at Alkmaar, are hardly adequate to balance the *forte* and *fortissimo* of the coupled tuttis of *Hauptwerk* and *Positiv*.

By the late sixteenth century the ingenuity of German builders was being devoted to technical developments apparently unrelated to the needs of contemporary composition. The besetting snare of builders has usually been the desire to excite wonder at the latest technical advances in their instruments. Often, though, this has coincided with a decline in the quality of the music prompted by the new technological marvels.

Praetorius gives detailed lists and descriptions of the tonal resources of the early seventeenth-century organs in his *Syntagma* of 1619, but apart from partitas and sets of chorale variations it is not easy to see how the tremendous variety of colour could be used in the available literature. One fruitful development in the experimentation with complex layouts of chests was the use of more than one chest for a division, thus enabling registrations to be prepared on a chest but not winded until a valve was released. The later ventil system of Cavaillé-Coll, in which the reed choruses were so separated, was to exert a potent influence on the registrational techniques of the romantic French school.

The nineteenth century witnessed the growing desire for larger, more powerful and more flexible instruments, involving the use of higher wind pressures together with all possibilities of coupling. Lighter actions were needed for the new pianistic textures which were gradually entering organ composition through the works of Mendelssohn, Schumann and Liszt. This led to the gradual abandonment of mechanical action, although it was sometimes retained for manuals but not for the more widely separated Pedal chests.

The Barker Lever
The idea of using a small bellows to pull down the pallet

21

and thereby remove the weight required to move the key was developed in England, most successfully by C.S. Barker from 1833 onwards, and his 'Barker lever' was taken up by Cavaillé-Coll for his St Denis instrument. This mechanical-pneumatic action retained the feel of precision from key to pipe, but did not allow physical control of the speed of opening and closing of the pallet.

In gaining pianistic lightness of touch, even with three manuals coupled, the player had to sacrifice subtlety of phrasing and articulation. Yet, because the mechanical element of trackers was retained, the console had to be placed in its traditional location in relation to the pipes. When the mechanical element was lost in favour of tubular-pneumatic action, which used a tube from key to pipe, the possibility of detached consoles and organs with widely separated chests proved to be irresistibly attractive, winning special favour in England and America.

But these actions were soon found to be slow and sluggish with the mechanical element removed, and it is not without significance that they found little approval in France, a country which was rapidly finding a new romantic literature of great significance under the joint inspiration of Franck and Cavaillé-Coll, based on a virtuoso approach to performance and therefore needing the precise response of piano action.

In England and America, the home of technological progress, interest centred mainly on the development of an entirely new kind of organ – both tonally and structurally – based on the new orchestral ideals of Strauss and Elgar, an instrument that fully reflected the rapidly developing organ engineering. The repertoire was based on orchestral transcriptions and J.S. Bach, whose music was given the full orchestral treatment so appropriate to late-Victorian ideas of artistic progress. Weight of tone and variety of colour were the all-important factors. Delicacy of articulation and phrasing, together with clarity of texture, were hardly considered.

The defects of tubular-pneumatic action were eventually recognized, once the fascination of divided instruments and detached consoles had run its course, and the application of electricity to actions appeared to be the obvious solution to sluggishness. Although 'direct electric action' had been used for small unit-chest organs, the electric-pneumatic action proved to be the most convenient and effective and it is usually this action that is loosely called 'electric' to this day. An early instance of its use was by Barker in the organ at St Augustin in Paris.

The Electric Organ

A good electric-pneumatic action is as prompt as a mechanical action (allowing for any time-lag caused by the distance of the pipes from the console) and it makes possible the widest separation of the divisions of the organ. A good example is the State Trumpet placed at the west end of the Cathedral of St John the Divine in New York. Many similar, if less spectacular, schemes are to be found all over the world, but once the novelty has worn off the purely musical possibilities are seen to be limited, and as nothing compared with the effect of a well-cased organ in which the sound is focused and projected from clearly located divisions within the casework, and controlled by a finely responsive, entirely mechanical action. If such an instrument has to be restricted in size, compared with the nineteenth-century monsters, the gain still far outweighs any loss for pre-nineteenth-century music.

Organ Touch

Anton Heiller once remarked that 'If there is anything worse than a bad electric organ, it is a good electric organ.' In other words, there is still an impassible gulf between the many good electric-action organs and those that give the player control over the opening speed of the pallet and therefore over the production of the sound – the varied attack and release that reflects the variety of good diction in speech. The technique of controlling the speed of the opening of the pallet must be acquired by means of the most careful listening to the onset of the sound and the relation of this to the 'feel' of the key movement.

For a player who comes to a responsive tracker-action instrument after years spent playing either sluggish pneumatic actions or electric actions with such a distance between pipes and keys as to make a time-lag inevitable, the experience will involve not only a revelation, but a re-education. Such a player will have spent those previous years either consciously or unconsciously training himself to neglect his ears in favour of his fingers and not to expect a correlation between touch and hearing. A responsive mechanical instrument returns the controlling factor firmly to where it is with every other instrument: the ear.

Study of this technique will involve the following considerations:

The character of individual ranks of pipes, used either by themselves or in chorus;

The character of the music for which the registration has been selected;

The relationship of each note to the rest of the note-group or phrase.

The precise clarity of attack and release is comparable to harpsichord technique where the plucking of the string marks the entry of each note in the way of an accent and the falling of the damper puts an equally abrupt stop to it. This is the reason why an almost mathematical regularity in the sequence of the notes is necessary. Eta Heinrich-Schneider has written that 'On no other instrument are rhythmical sloppiness and irregular finger action so painfully audible as on the harpsichord,' but this is equally true of the organ. Whereas the tone of the harpsichord is unaffected by the kind of attack the player uses, the mechanical action of the organ can be compared in this respect more with the touch of the pianist, where the speed of the hammer striking the string is responsible for the kind of tone produced.

Organ touch may therefore be said to lie somewhere

between that needed for the harpsichord and that needed for the piano. The similarities with harpsichord touch lie in the required precision of attack and release, together with every variety of legato, non-legato or *détaché* and staccato. As with the piano, the speed of key movement influences the attack, giving the organist something like the pianist's control of tone production.

Apart from the keyboard, the only shared feature, the organ has nothing in common with the harpsichord and piano. It is essentially a large wind instrument, depending on wind or breath, as does the human voice, and the characteristics of its music will be those of vocal and wind-instrumental music. In view of this it is not surprising to find that the earliest sources of organ music include transcriptions of vocal motets and that the legato style and phrasing inseparable from vocal music are the basis of organ-playing.

Legato

Speaking generally of harpsichord technique, Couperin says, 'A perfect legato must be preserved in all that is executed upon it.' If this is true of an instrument generally regarded as being so deficient in sustaining power, how much more important this will be for the organ! 'Make the instrument sing' must be the aim for an instrument that derives so much of its repertoire from vocal sources.

A singing legato, however perfect, involves breathing (phrasing in all voices) and consonants as well as vowels (varied articulation and attack). It certainly does not mean a constant, gluey, unbroken sound, without musical sense of shape. Rhythmic organization, as opposed to metrical organization, will be conveyed by articulation. The down-beat must be clearly established, then a hierarchy of the other beats. If the attack of a note is its most important aspect, then the crucial role of mechanical action in its achievement is obvious.

Couperin's 'perfect legato' is then only the beginning of good organ-playing, on any type of action. Because non-mechanical actions are not capable of varied control of the pallet opening – and the resulting subtlety of articulation – the most detailed attention to the alteration of note values in order to simulate accentuation is necessary. However, even with the most responsive mechanical action, the full legato should be regarded as one technique among many and not as the accepted norm.

When a singer sings perfectly smoothly – unless a level, uniform effect is required for some particular reason – there will be a variety of tone and accent in the voice. This variety of sound has to be simulated on the organ by constant variety of touch. For this reason the basic norm of organ touch should be the 'balanced' or 'clear' legato: that which results from the degree of connection possible when playing repeated notes. Scales played with perfect legato, followed by an exercise on repeated notes, and with this technique then applied to the scales will establish the correct method.

With this technique firmly established as the normal organ touch, the problem of historically appropriate styles of articulation can be considered. With this must go the study of fingering.

Fingering and Articulation
The fact that in pre-eighteenth century music the thumb and fifth fingers were rarely used gives some guide as to the type of articulation appropriate for early music. The wholesale adoption of early fingering would not be feasible for players today unless they intended to specialize in the early repertoire, but the study of it is essential if an insight into correct articulation is to be gained.

The main point is that a purely 'comfortable' or 'convenient' fingering, often arrived at with little consideration of alternative methods, is not necessarily, or even usually, the best one for the music of any period, and this is specially true for baroque and pre-baroque music. The music and its phrasing and articulation should be studied before reading it through at the keyboard, when careless and ill-considered habits of fingering are easily formed. Although it is clearly not true to say that early keyboard music lacked its own idiom, it is true that figurations and articulations from wind- and string-playing techniques were quickly imitated and assimilated into keyboard styles.

The main difference between the articulation of keyboard music before and after 1800 is in the individuality of the notes. The semiquavers in Titelouze and Sweelinck, for example, must be allowed to breathe and have their own life within the motive or figurative pattern. They have a structural function in the musical design, however tiny, whereas in Liszt or Reger groups of semiquavers may have a colouristic function, and may need to be played clearly but not given the precise identity necessary in early music.

Among romantic composers for the organ Mendelssohn is an interesting case of a mid-point idiom. The finales from his First and Fifth Sonatas make an interesting comparison. The toccata-like textures of the First need a baroque-like clarity of articulation, the semiquaver figuration carrying the substance of the structure, whereas in the last movement of the Fifth the quaver triplets have a harmonic and accompanimental function quite different from the Bach Prelude in C minor (BWV 546) which was the obvious model for the movement.

Whereas the same type of articulative treatment seems to be appropriate for music from Bull to Buxtehude, when we turn to Bach and Handel, with their indebtedness to the Italian string school of Corelli and Vivaldi, we have to look very carefully at their writing for strings and wind in order to see what musical effect they intend to produce. Bowing and phrasing indications are much more common in the instrumental works than are phrasings in the keyboard music, where the few indications appear to be a guide to do other than would normally be expected. (A good example is to be found in the last movement of Bach's Trio Sonata No. 6.)

Once again, Mendelssohn is revealing. In the last movement of his Second Sonata his use of slurs in the fugue

subject can mean only bowing-like articulations, not
phrase marks. A later edition by Ivor Atkins replaced
these markings by legato phrasings – a good illustration of
early twentieth-century misunderstanding of true organ
style, a style that still looked back to the eighteenth
century.

When we think of bowing as a guide to the articulation of
Bach's keyboard music we need to remember that this was
as different from romantic bowings as early keyboard
articulation was from the figurations of Chopin and Liszt.
As a powerful melodic line with accompaniment began to
dominate instrumental textures in the course of the nineteenth century, smoothness of texture became prized
above all else. In order to achieve this perfect legato the
technique of finger substitution was cultivated. Although
appropriate for some Mendelssohn movements – mostly
the slow, lyrical ones – and for Franck, when the same
technique was applied to Bach the results were disastrous.

Just as an incessant legato from the fingers is wrong for
Bach, so the over-use of the heels in pedalling militates
against the clear articulation of the pedal line. Instead, the
use of toes only for much of the time makes the detached
style of playing required for early music quite convincing.
Just as early keyboards make the turning of the thumb
virtually impossible, so the short, flat pedal boards of the
same time make it clear that heels were used very spar-
ingly. The crossing of feet is also to be avoided as there is
evidence that the technique was new as late as 1750.

We need now to consider the basic criteria for determin-
ing articulation in differing styles of organ music: the legato
'singing' style for sustained, vocally inspired textures; the
clear or balanced legato for animated lines, and varying
degrees of *détaché* and staccato. With regard to the 'clear'
legato, the words of Friedrich Marpurg are worth pon-
dering. In his *Die Kunst, das Klavier zu spielen* of 1750 he
writes, 'Contrasted with legato as well as with staccato
playing is the ordinary progression in which one quickly
raises the finger from the preceding key just before striking

a new key. Because this ordinary method is always assumed, it is never indicated.'

This 'clear' legato in organ-playing corresponds to the 'ordinary method' of separate bows in baroque string-playing. Both techniques ensure the individuality of the notes but it should be remembered that the string-player still has the advantage over the organist in that he can obtain a variety of accentuation by dynamic means. So we must decide in every bar and phrase which are the accented and which the unaccented notes – 'heavy' or 'light' – and then establish their hierarchy.

It will be useful to bear in mind that:

> Conjunct notes are legato, either 'clear' or slurred;
> Notes in leaps are detached to some degree;
> Accent is produced by shortening notated values before the required accent; or, in slow, sustained music, by a combination of slight shortening and lengthening of the appropriate values; or, where no detaching would be appropriate, a careful lengthening of the notes will produce the simulation of accent.

Examples from Bach and Vierne will demonstrate the principles involved. However, these alterations are so subtle that signs can be regarded only as a rough and approximate guide to the desired result, just as analytic techniques can function only as a partial stage towards a fuller perception of the music itself.

A comparison of three different articulations of the fugue subject from Bach's Prelude and Fugue in G (BWV 541) is instructive. Schweitzer's characteristic slurring from weak to strong on the second and third beats in common time produces an incorrect effect of syncopation. For some reason he failed to appreciate how this procedure destroyed all possibility of a correct simulated accent on the organ. Dupré's interpretation follows Schweitzer in basic approach and neither attempts to relate Bach's organ version of the theme with that in his *Cantata 21*. My version does, providing the slurs are regarded as implying a 'clear' legato touch. The vigorous accentuation that the German

Organ

J.S. Bach: Fugue in G minor (BWV 541)

Schweitzer

Dupré

J.S. Bach: Cantata 21

Ich hat - te viel Be - küm-mer- nis, ich hat-te viel Be - küm-mer-niss in mei-nem

'Clear' legato in slurred figures

Wills

text gives to this phrase is precisely the model needed for its correct articulation on the organ.

The excerpts from Vierne are just as illuminating. Here we have a very sustained line in which both the curve of the melody and the impossibility of *détaché* militate against the accurate aural perception of the rhythmic organization. The only way to convey the correct rhythm is by slightly lengthening the first note in each bar.

Choral

Vierne: Symphonie II

Ped.

30

Generally speaking the degree of articulation adopted must obviously depend on the tempo decided for the music, and this in turn will be greatly influenced by the acoustic of the room as well as by the action of the instrument and the voicing of the pipes. Clarity of both rhythm and texture is the paramount factor in organ-playing. It is harder to achieve than on any other instrument and therefore presents a challenge to the player to develop his artistry to the full – an ever-present source of both elation and despair.

Three
'In the Beginning ... '

Antiquity

Much of the history of the organ before the fourteenth century is necessarily conjectural, and this is even more true of the music that would have been performed. However, conjecture can be stimulating and may even help our understanding of the relationship between the instrument's origins and early development and its later, more fully documented, history and may possibly contribute to our perception of its basic nature and purpose.

The Hydraulus

The invention of the first 'organ' is usually ascribed to a Greek engineer, Ktesibios, who worked in Alexandria around 250 BC. The Hydraulus (water organ), a remarkable machine or 'tool', represented a peak of achievement in Greek technology of the period, but nothing is known of its use in Greek culture.

It was taken up by the Romans, who appreciated its powerful tone for use in vast arenas. Its main function was to entertain audiences at such events as circuses and gladiator combats, as well as to provide an appropriate accompaniment for the activities of various religious cults. Clearly it must have been valued chiefly for its unique penetrative tone, derived from the simultaneous sounding of several ranks of different pitches, controlled by the action of one key.

W. H. Auden's poetic insight aptly voices our vision of the organ at this time in his 'Song for St Cecilia's Day':

> this innocent virgin
> Constructed an organ to enlarge her prayer,
> And notes tremendous from her great engine
> Thundered out on the Roman air.

The idea of the organ as an imitation orchestra has persisted, probably reaching its high point in the early years of the twentieth century.

From the outset, the triple fascination of the instrument is clear. First, there is the sheer volume of sound that can be produced by one player – much greater and more varied than that from any other solo instrumentalist, or combination of performers. Second, there is the irresistible combination of high art and advanced technology – the Hydraulus must be considered one of the greatest achievements of ancient engineering. Third, there is the attractive economy of putting this amount of tonal power in the hands of a single performer, who could easily rival and possibly outdo the sound available from any orchestral group known to the ancient world.

In this intriguing example of early engineering, the Hydraulus, the basic nature of the organ can be clearly seen. A wind chest is divided into channels on each of which stands a number of pipes of different pitches. These pipes sound simultaneously when the appropriate key is activated. The wind is supplied by a bellows and the pressure stabilized and maintained by the hydraulic principle. In essence, the organ has not changed over two thousand years.

Although its usefulness as a substitute for other instruments was recognized from the beginning, and although the development of the instrument was to be on strongly imitative lines – ranks based on flute, oboe, trumpet and trombone timbres and so on – the origins were clearly those of an inimitable sonority, the chorus of many pitches.

This characteristic was progressively ignored towards the end of the nineteenth century when the recently evolved romantic orchestra became the model for organ sonority, and it has taken a good part of the twentieth century for it to be once again fully appreciated and reflected in organ-building and in performance practice. The perennial dual use of the instrument, both for mass entertainment and for more esoteric functions, has dogged the history of the organ up to our own times, in which we still experience the conflicting claims of the church and the town hall or cinema.

The relatively inert quality of the sound produced by a mechanically derived wind pressure makes it obvious that the subtlety which an individual wind-player might obtain from his instrument was never implicit in the early origins of the organ. No dynamic variation or shading of the tone was possible. It was, and still is, essentially an instrument for broad effects. This is especially true of the Principal division of the organ in large buildings. We shall see how smaller instruments, capable of greater delicacy and flexibility, evolved and were eventually integrated with larger instruments to offer the potential for both breadth and intimacy.

Four
The Middle Ages

The potential for expanding the size and power of the ancient Hydraulus was not lost on the early Church, and St Hieronymous' mention (c.AD 400) of an organ at Jerusalem that could be heard at the Mount of Olives, almost a mile distant, is well known. (Similar stories persist in all periods. There is an equally well-known and frequently corroborated claim that the Ely organ can be heard from the railway station.)

It was natural that the building of the immense Gothic cathedrals should be matched by the provision of organs of a comparable size and ingenuity. Perhaps the most famous is the Winchester Cathedral organ, built in the late tenth century. It had 400 pipes, two manuals of twenty notes each – with slides, not keys – and twenty-six pairs of bellows worked by 'seventy strong men'. It required two performers to operate the slides, and as each slide sounded ten pipes the resulting sonority was overwhelming. As Wulfstan (d.c.963) says, 'Everyone stops with his hands his gaping ears, being in no wise able to draw near and bear the sound.' Early accounts of organs are often dismissed as examples of gross poetic exaggeration, but it is not unreasonable to suppose that these writers desired and imagined a sonority that seemed to them a fitting match for the architectural splendours arising around them.

Slider Action

It is curious that the subtlety of using stops to isolate

different ranks, although known to the Greek builders and throughout the ancient world, was not developed in the medieval organs of western Europe until very late in the period. Similarly, the advanced key action of the Hydraulus was replaced by cumbersome slides. The absence of stops, and therefore of individually sounding ranks, in the western medieval organ established its fundamental character from the beginning – the basic sound of the organ is not that of a single 8' Diapason or Principal; it is rather a chorus of several pitches.

The slider action meant that the medieval organ was ponderous in execution, however impressive in tone, and its precise function is far from certain. The normal position appears to have been in close proximity to the voices and it may have been used to sustain the long tenor notes in the performance of organa, but its powerful sonority would not have blended with a small number of voices. It was more likely to have had a solo function, used either in alternation with the choral music in improvised versets, or to adorn otherwise silent parts of the liturgy. None of this can be proved. The crude slider mechanism was gradually superseded, during the eleventh, twelfth and thirteenth centuries, by the re-invention of the keyboard. The instrument was thereby revolutionized, and the vastly increased flexibility of execution led to its becoming very popular both for church and domestic use.

The *Blockwerk*, the Portative, the Positive and Regal

Organs were now built in a great variety of dimensions, according to their intended usage, and four main types became common:

The Mixture Organ or *Blockwerk*, a large instrument for important monastic and abbey churches, sounding several pitches, perhaps from three to ten, for each key. Some large cathedrals preferred to have several smaller instruments placed round the building for different liturgical occasions.

Portatives, with one rank of pipes, which could be played in processional movement (not unlike the modern piano accordian), or placed on a table. Their use was mainly melodic and useful both in the church and the home.

Positives, of one or more ranks, usually flute tone. A typical example is illustrated in the Belvoir Psalter of *c.*1270. Too large to be easily moved, they were built in a wide variety of sizes and were used as liturgical instruments.

The Regal was introduced around 1450 and remained in use for some two hundred years. It was a small instrument of reeds without pipes which, like the Portative, could be placed on a table or provided with its own supports and clearly anticipates features of the much later harmonium.

Some churches preferred to have several Positives of different sizes in preference to the unwieldy *Blockwerk*. Durham, for instance, had five organs by the end of the sixteenth century. Certainly, after the Reformation, developments in England were centred on a moderate-sized organ, suitable for choral accompaniment, as opposed to the Continental tradition of larger instruments more appropriate to the splendour of the Catholic liturgy or the congregational requirements of the Reformed Church.

The Positive remained popular until the eighteenth century and the last significant repertoire to be composed for it was Handel's organ concertos. Interest in the instrument waned with nineteenth-century concentration on the developing orchestral organ, but the Positive has been revived during the last twenty-five years, sometimes with rather odd stop lists. The Positive concept brought to the organ delicate and intimate textures, as well as sparkling brilliance, and its eventual incorporation, as a second division, into the *Blockwerk*, was to be of far-reaching importance for the development of organ music.

Although the most recent research makes it impossible

to be more than highly conjectural in detail, it is broadly true to say that the development of the organ from 1450 onwards was concerned mainly with the expansion and amalgamation of the *Blockwerk*, the Positive and the Regal. The *Blockwerk*, the 'mixture chorus' organ, was enriched by the vital invention of the stop – a device that separated certain ranks and introduced the possibility of variety of sound by using two or three combinations and, eventually, separate ranks. The broad-toned Principal chorus developed from this innovation.

The Positive was enlarged from the original one or two ranks in order to suit the building and use for which it was intended. This type, in which every rank was separable, was developed south of the Alps, and early examples may still be found in Italy. After the invention of the stop on the *Blockwerk*, and the enlargement of the separate-rank Positive, the next step was to bring both the large and the small instruments under the control of one performer, thereby vastly increasing the range of sonorities, and providing the possibility of contrast between the breadth of tone of the *Blockwerk* and the lively brilliance and precise delicacy of the Positive. This newly acquired characteristic of the instrument was to become a potent source of inspiration to composers.

Allowing for over-simplification of a very uncertain train of events, it would appear that early experiments placed the two instruments in convenient juxtaposition with the keyboards facing one another and the seat in between. Even when the two keyboards were eventually located together it was common to leave the stop-levers positioned behind the player.

The Robertsbridge Codex

The absence of flexibility of tone and execution in the large medieval *Blockwerk* clearly precluded any development of a specifically instrumental style, and it is not surprising to find that the earliest extant collection of keyboard music (*c*.1325) is contemporary with the emergence of the Positive organ. This is the Robertsbridge Codex, and the four complete pieces it contains in tablature consist of two versions of motets and two dances, or estampies. So, the origins of organ music are found in song and dance – the basis of all structured music. Sacred song and secular dance: this bedrock of the repertoire may still be found in a Messiaen *méditation* or a Vierne scherzo.

It is possible that the music of the Robertsbridge Codex might also have been played upon the Echiquier, most probably the first keyboard instrument to have strings. From the earliest times, the development of the organ and of other keyboard instruments proceeded together, with the accumulation of a shared repertoire. This intimate connection between keyboard instruments lasted into the high baroque era (J. S. Bach's keyboard music) and beyond into the romantic period (the Schumann pieces for pedal piano, and two of Liszt's major keyboard works in versions for both piano and organ).

The Robertsbridge Codex makes an excellent start for a pianist of Grade V or VI standard who wishes to begin organ studies. Delightful as these pieces are, they immediately confront the student with the essential problems of organ-playing. Two are vocal, raising the question of phrasing, which is where instrumentalists can learn from singers; and two are dances, concerned with vital rhythm and the articulation of short motives. To get to grips with these problems we need to compare (a) the respective keyboard techniques of piano and organ; and (b) the difference between a wind instrument such as an oboe or a flute, and a set of pipes on a wind-chest.

These first pieces of organ music necessitate the student grasping the importance of duration, timing, the alteration of the composer's values to obtain rhythmic articulation and accent – all in order to be able to make the instrument sing, dance, and do both together.

Two of the Robertsbridge pieces aptly illustrate this.

Organ

The fifth is an intabulation of a motet, 'Tribum quem', and the second is a lively and attractive estampie. Both pieces require considerable agility and clear definition of rapid figuration and were almost certainly intended for a Positive organ. Flute tone of 8' and 2' pitch suits both pieces well.

The estampie requires an articulated legato touch and no more. This is the equivalent of a wind-player's 'tonguing' and assists the rhythmic vitality which is essential to this dance music. The conjunct motive

♩ ♪♩ ♪ may be effectively slurred ♩ ♪♩ ♪

The required overall effect is of well-pointed rhythm and sparkling approach. I suggest a metronome mark

♩. = 116

The motet needs a smoother approach and the decorative figuration of the upper voice must not be allowed to obscure an overall sense of line. The groups of six semiquavers may be played

i.e., three with slurred legato, followed by three detached. These need only slight separation, but this careful judgement of duration is certainly basic to good organ phrasing. Let this motet flow gently – a metronome mark of

♩ = 60

would be appropriate.

Five
The Renaissance

Germany and the Netherlands

Notable developments in organ-building took place in Germany and the Netherlands, and by the end of the fourteenth century instruments with two or three manuals and a short-compass pedal board, such as that built in 1361 at Halberstadt in Germany, were becoming familiar. Within a hundred years the type of organ we now recognize as 'North German' had established itself.

The third manual was usually a Regal division, positioned in the main case as a *Brustwerk*, and often confined to the treble range. The different divisions of an organ were frequently assembled over a long period: the well-known Totentanz organ of Lübeck, destroyed in 1942, is a case in point. The Totentanz had a fifteenth-century Great Organ, a sixteenth-century Chair Organ, a seventeenth-century *Brustwerk*, and its Pedal Organ was enlarged in the eighteenth century.

Two fifteenth-century German publications are of importance, both for what they reveal about the art of the organ at this period, and for their value as playing material (which is particularly useful for a beginner).

The *Fundamentum organisandi* (1452) by Conrad Paumann (*c*.1410–1473) is included in a manuscript with the Lochamer Liederbuch. As Paumann uses popular songs as the basis of his pieces, we can assume that they were intended for domestic use on a Portative or small Positive Organ. His book is in effect a treatise on the contrapuntal elaboration of such material.

A version of the *Fundamentum organisandi* is also to be found in the more important Buxheimer Orgelbuch (*c*.1470) which contains 256 pieces, both liturgical and secular. Pieces arranged from vocal works dominate the Buxheimer collection, but some short preambles or preludes are included, and these are the first free compositions we have.

They alternate freely running melodic passages with chordal sections in an improvisatory style that clearly points to J. S. Bach's Fantasia in G minor (BWV 542). The collection also contains hymns and mass movements intended to alternate with the plainsong on which they are based. This is a technique brought to a glorious culmination in the works of Nicolas de Grigny (1671–1703) and François Couperin (1668–1733) in seventeenth-century France.

The pieces in the Buxheimer Orgelbuch are mostly short and make a useful supplement to the Robertsbridge pieces. Many are only one page in length, and although not difficult in terms of technique they nevertheless present problems of rhythm and phrasing – all most useful for this stage of training. Modern editions use slurs to indicate structural phrasing, but subtlety of articulation within the phrase is needed if the music is to be projected with the necessary vitality. Slurs, staccato marks and all graphic notational aids can give only an approximate idea of what is required; the ear must be the final judge.

Christus Resurrexit (Buxheimer Orgelbuch No. 46)

Italy

Italian organ music developed rapidly, and several genres were established during this period which underlie organ composition to this day: the toccata, fantasia, ricercar and canzona. The toccata and the fantasia probably developed from the practice of improvisation, a skill required of every organist. The ricercar and the canzona were based on the vocal genres of chanson and motet. Both of these lie behind the fugue: the secular spirit of the rhythmically lively canzona contrasts with the church-like solemnity of the slow-moving ricercar, with its 'learned' contrapuntal devices of stretto, inversion and augmentation.

The canzonas of Girolamo Cavazzoni (*c.*1425 – *after* 1577) are well worth study, as are the ricercars of Andrea (1510–1586) and Giovanni Gabrieli (1557–1612) and the toccatas of Claudio Merulo (1533–1604), but the crowning achievement of Italian organ music is the work of Girolamo Frescobaldi (1583–1643).

The instrument in S. Giuseppe, Brescia, completed by Graziadio Antegnati in 1581, is typical of the Italian Renaissance organ. Comprising only Principals, Flutes and

---

S. GIUSEPPE, BRESCIA

CCDDEEFFGGAA–g″a″ (53 notes)

Principale	8 (halves)
Ottava	4
Quintadecima	2
Decimanona	$1\frac{1}{3}$
Vigesimaseconda	1
Vigesimasesta	$\frac{2}{3}$
Vigesimanona	$\frac{1}{2}$
Trigesimaterza	$\frac{1}{3}$
Trigesimasesta	$\frac{1}{4}$
Flauto in ottava	4
Flauto in duodecima	$2\frac{2}{3}$
Flauto in quintadecima	2
Fiffaro	8 (treble only)

Pedal pulldowns, this organ combines a glittering spread of pitches with a mellow sweetness of tone, due mainly to a low wind pressure of c.42mm.

The single-manual organs of northern Italy usually divided at middle C to enable the use of solo effects. The tutti of such an organ is merely a more refined version of the medieval *Blockwerk*, or a more fully developed Positive, the only innovation being the undulating (sharp), treble-compass Fiffaro. This would be drawn with the Principale for use in slow and expressive pieces, such as the toccatas 'per le levatione' in Frescobaldi's *Fiori musicale* of 1635. In his preface Frescobaldi instructs the player to 'find out the affection of the passage'; to use some variety of tempo 'in the madrigal manner'; to articulate rapid passages, and to ritard the cadences.

Guidance about registration is given in the books by Costanzo Antegnati and Adriano Banchieri. The severe ricercars require only unison pitches 8', 4' and 2'. The toccatas utilize the full sound of the tutti. The lively canzonas are best served by Flutes and the lighter Principales, while the Fiffaro should be reserved for the more intensely expressive pieces. The Pedal pulldown of the Italian instruments was probably used for long held notes in the more improvisatory type of piece, for which role they were clearly well suited.

France

Some of the earliest melodically independent use of the pedals is to be found in the two collections by Jean Titelouze (1563–1633). Both were intended for use at Vespers and consist of versets for Office hymns and Magnificats. The cantus firmus pedal, with 8' Flute and reed stops, was a fairly common feature in the French organ around 1600 and the texture of many of the versets makes it likely that its use was intended – most commonly in the bass or tenor line.

The French organ of the late Renaissance was strongly

influenced by Flemish models. An oft-quoted example is the instrument built by Nicolas Barbier at St-Gervais and St-Protais, Gisors, in 1580. The remarkably full specification was a prototype of the seventeenth-century French organ and the solo role of the Pedal division will be immediately apparent. Although a Pedal coupler is not mentioned, it would almost certainly have been provided for the *plein jeu* or Full Organ (the asterisked stops), in which the Pedal played the bass cantus firmus.

ST-GERVAIS AND ST-PROTAIS, GISORS

Grand Orgue		*Positif*	
CD–c'''		CD–c'''	
Montre	16*	Bourdon	8
Montre	8*	Prestant	4
Bourdon	8*	Doublette	2
Prestant	4*	Petite Quinte	1⅓
Flûte	4	Cymbale	II
Nasard	2⅔	Cromorne	8
Doublette	2*		
Sifflet	1	*Pédale*	
Fourniture	IV*	Jeu de pédale	8
Cymbale	III*	Sacquebouttes	8
Quint-flûte	1⅓		
Cornet	V		
Trompette	8		
Clairon	4		
Voix humaine	8	* *plein jeu*	

For the student, slow-moving melodic lines, played legato except for breathing spaces at the end of each line, make the best possible introduction, apart from purely technical exercises, to pedal playing. The hymn 'Iste confessor' is a good choice to begin with. When the pedal line is secure and fluent, the manual parts may be added gradually, beginning with the tenor part played with the left hand.

England

Documentation of English organs is scant until the seventeenth century, but the available sources suggest that the earliest instruments were influenced by the work of Dutch and Flemish builders. Under Puritan influence after the Reformation, churches were not prepared to spend money on organs, and the English Renaissance organ was usually a Positive of about six stops.

The best source of organ music we have from this period is the Mulliner Book. This is another most useful compilation for a first-year student, ranging from pieces that could be used at the first lesson, such as the Voluntary by Richard Farrant (c.1530–1580) (No. 20), to such demanding works as the *Gloria tibi Trinitas* pieces by William Blitheman (d.1591) (Nos. 92–5). Compiled for use in St Paul's Cathedral during the second half of the sixteenth century, the Mulliner Book contains a wide variety of pieces, sacred and secular, transcriptions and original material, thus continuing the comprehensive nature of such collections as the Robertsbridge Codex and the *Fiori musicale* of Frescobaldi.

Music for church and chamber organ reached new heights in the work of such masters as John Bull (c.1562–1628), William Byrd (c.1542–1623) and Orlando Gibbons (1583–1625) and was influential in the development of keyboard music on the Continent, especially in the work of Sweelinck and his pupils, through whom a direct route to the music of J. S. Bach can be traced.

Sweelinck

Jan Sweelinck (1562–1621) was known as 'the maker of German organists' since many of his pupils became prominent players and composers all over northern Europe. Among them were Heinrich Scheidemann (c.1596–1663), Michael Praetorius (1571–1621) and, most notably, Samuel Scheidt (1587–1654). Sweelinck and Scheidt used pieces by John Dowland (1563–1626) and Peter Philips (*c*.1561–1628) as the basis of sets of variations, and Bull repaid this compliment with his *Fantasia on a Theme by Sweelinck* (1621).

Some of Sweelinck's pieces were included in the Fitz-william Virginal Book and he had studied the techniques of the English virginal composers carefully. He adopted the patterned variation type and used this with both folk and chorale melodies. The German Reformed Church had produced a chorale book, with sources based on rhythmic-ized versions of plainsong and some secular material. These were used in a cantus firmus style, similar to that used by the Catholic school of composers in France and Italy. Italian influence is to be found in his toccatas, fantasias and ricercars as well as in his use of chromaticism.

The organ in the Oude Kerk, Amsterdam, was known to Sweelinck. It was built by Hendrik and Hermann Niehoff, with Hans Suys, in 1539–42 and modified in 1544. There was plenty of variety on the manuals for partitas and

OUDE KERK, AMSTERDAM

Prinzipal		*Oberwerk*	
Probably FGA–g"a"		F–a"	
Prinzipal	16	Prinzipal	8
Oktave	8 + 4	Holpijp	8
Mixtur		Offenflöte	4
Scharf		Quintadena	4
Rückpositiv		Gemshorn	2
F–a"		Sifflöte	1 or 1⅓
Prinzipal	8	Zimbel	III
Oktave	4	Trompete	8
Mixtur		Zinck (treble)	8
Scharf			
Quintadena	8	*Pedal*	
Holpijp	4	FGA–c'	
Krummhorn	8		
Regal	8	Nachthorn	2
Baarpijp	8	Trompete	8
Schalmei	4	Coupler: *Prinzipal/Pedal*	

variations and the Pedal department could either be coupled to the Prinzipal manual or used as a strong solo line in chorale melodies. The tonal quality was gentle and singing, rather than forceful and brilliant, a quality more typical of the baroque organ of the seventeenth century.

The influence of the Oude Kerk design on the Gisors organ is immediately apparent, and, apart from the Pedal division, it could serve as a model for the large 'town church' instruments of Arp Schnitger, over a century later. The relationship of music and organ is obvious and Sweelinck's use of the patterned variation technique was ideally suited to the baroque doctrine of the 'affections'.

The study of Sweelinck's music follows on naturally from that of the English School and Titelouze. The pedal lines are more flexible than those of Titelouze and the use of manual changes within a movement is introduced in the 'echo' fantasias. The variation pieces offer useful practice in the choice of varied and appropriate registrations.

Spain

The Spanish organ of the Renaissance was slow to acquire national characteristics, and the builders were usually either from Italy or the Netherlands. Two obvious differences were in the feature of an internal Positive, rather than a Chair Organ, and the presence of rather more mixtures than would be found in an Italian instrument. There is an emphasis on colourful reeds: 'Clarins de galera' and 'Clarins de mar' hint at things to come. Also plentiful are 'toy' effects – drums, nightingales, Zimbelstern, a plethora of tremulants.

But if a capacity for flamboyance was typical of a mid-sixteenth-century Spanish organ, the greatest composer of the period, Antonio de Cabezón (c.1500–1566), was remarkable for his reserved and austere musical personality. His liturgical music is essentially vocal in inspiration and style, and he produced several intabulations or glosas of existing motets and chansons, an example being Josquin's *Ave Maria*. The tiento was much cultivated at this period; a piece in strict imitative counterpoint for much of the time, and virtually synonymous with the ricercar or fantasia.

The Renaissance repertoire, with its predominantly vocal basis, and sparing use of the pedal, gives the student a good grounding in the concept of the organ as a singing instrument. The player needs to strive for the subtle smoothness of a first-rate choir in the independent phrasing of the voices; a sense of rhythmic articulation (the equivalent of vocal consonants) and a feeling for verbal emphasis and colour in chordal passages.

Six
The Golden Age:
The Seventeenth Century

Appreciation of the music of the seventeenth century is a fairly recent phenomenon. At the beginning of this century Sir Hubert Parry could write, 'The seventeenth century is, musically, almost a blank.' Greater familiarity with the music in performance has brought increasing respect and love, and now seventeenth-century music almost rivals the music of the nineteenth and twentieth centuries in interest and popularity.

After the relatively stable and ordered Renaissance era, the experimental and innovatory aspects of the period are inclined to overshadow actual achievement. The almost feverish atmosphere of change and exploration is remarkably reminiscent of the start of the twentieth century. Yet this turbulent age witnessed – at any rate in Germany and France – a period of remarkable achievements in the evolution of the organ, both in the technology of construction and in the repertoire.

The early years of the seventeenth century show a gradual transformation of Renaissance style. Fully developed, contrapuntal pieces, in a stable, ordered idiom, give way to more sectionally constructed works, with much more emphasis on colour and drama. This trend away from the orderly, calm and developed art of such composers as Giovanni Palestrina (c.1525–1594) and Gibbons, and towards such agitated and experimental composers as Claudio Monteverdi (1567–1643) and Dietrich Buxtehude (1637–1707) was formerly regarded as evidence of uncertainty of purpose and inferiority of achievement. Now the period is seen as having produced some of the most innovative, expressive and stimulating music in the whole history of the art.

Music as an expression of the individual consciousness began to emerge, led by the new genre of opera. The solo voice was matched by the solo instrument as a source of expression and virtuosity. On the organ solo stops rather than pedals gave prominence to a cantus firmus.

The French school was notable for the fresh emphasis it gave to colour. The Dutch–North German school was not untouched by this development, but concentrated rather along the lines of highly developed contrapuntal structures, mainly under the influence of Sweelinck and his pupils, culminating in the work of Johann Sebastian Bach (1685–1750).

The fact that the greatest composer of the baroque period was also the greatest composer of organ music is, of course, no mere coincidence. As M. F. Bukofzker says, 'In Germany, the organ was afforded the highest rank in the hierarchy of instruments.' This is not surprising when we remember the German predilection for contrapuntal writing. Of all instruments, the organ gives the solo player the maximum opportunity for the richest and most varied of contrapuntal textures.

The Werkprinzip

Although the basic principles of the German baroque or *Werkprinzip* organ were known by the beginning of the fifteenth century, they were to be fully developed only during the period 1550–1750. The Oude Kerk organ has already been discussed; equally important for our understanding of the evolution of the instrument at this period is the Hofkirche organ at Innsbruck. Built by G. Ebert in 1555–61 and restored by Jürgen Ahrend in 1970, it is, in Peter Williams's opinion, 'without doubt one of the most important organs in the world'.

Its position is unique as the oldest extant two-manual

HOFKIRCHE, INNSBRUCK

Hauptwerk		Rückpositiv	
CDEFGA–g″a″		FGA–g″a″	
Prinzipal	8	Prinzipal	4
Gedackt	8	Gedackt	4
Oktave	4	Mixtur	III–V
Quinte	2⅔	Hörnlein	II (new)
Superoktave	2	Zimbel	II (new)
Hörnlein	II		
Hintersatz	V–X	Pedal	
Zimbel	II	CDEFGA–bb	
Trompete	8 (new)	Operating own row of pallets	
Regal	8 (new)	in Hw chest	

organ in the world, and it is the relationship of the two keyboards that makes it so fascinating. The *Rückpositiv* largely duplicates the *Hauptwerk* an octave higher, as if the two divisions were conceived as separations and extensions of one unified chorus. Looked at in this way the idea can be seen as a development of the Italian single manual with half-stops. Contrast of pitch, rather than tone, would appear to have been the aim, and this was to be reflected in the pitch structure of many later Positives. The unified sound from both keyboards (with the spatial separation of a Chair Organ) alerts us to the idea that pitch and spatial separation are more important to an organ than simple tonal contrast.

The *Werkprinzip* instrument follows the natural evolution of the medieval organ; to the main case is added the *Positiv* or Chair Organ, and then separate pedal-towers. This is the purest form of the *Werkprinzip*, but many, and sometimes less satisfactory, variants were derived from it.

The essence of the *Werkprinzip* is that of two balanced but contrasting manuals, the depth and richness of the Great Organ pitted against the brilliance and immediacy of the *Positiv* – this is the solo manual, both in character and siting, at once assertive and expressive. The Great Organ and the Chair Organ complement each other. They have separate identities and yet are perfectly harmonious in chorus. Each is firmly underpinned by a Pedal division of equal clarity and independence – except in the tutti of coupled manuals, when pedal couplers need to be drawn.

The *Werkprinzip* instrument reached its highest point of evolution in the work of Arp Schnitger (1648–1719). His organ at Uithuizen, built in 1701, makes a useful comparison with the Amsterdam and Innsbruck instruments. It was modified by P. van Oeckelen in 1854–5 but it is the contract specification that is reproduced here.

The *Werkprinzip* organ would have been known by Buxtehude and the Bach family and was still suitable for the music of Sweelinck and his disciples. The work of Scheidt is a natural development of Sweelinck's, in the way it uses the *Werkprinzip* organ, and specially for the varied

---

UITHUIZEN

Manuaal		*Rugh Positijf*	
Praestant	8	Praestant	8
Hollpijp	8	Gedackt	8
Octavo	4	Quintadena	8
Floyt	4	Hollpijp	4
Quinta	3	Sexquialter	2
Super Octavo	2	Octavo	2
Suflet	1½	Walt Floyt	2
Mixtuer	IV–V	Quinta	1½
Trompet	8	Scharp	4
Vox Humana	8	Dulciaan	8

Pedael	
Bourdon	16
Octavo	8
Octavo	4
Nachthoorn	2
Mixtuer	4
Basuijn	16
Trompet	8
Cornet	2

Marmaelkappel, Tremulant, 4 Blaasbalgen

---

use of the Pedal division. In his preface to his *Tabulatura nova* of 1624 Scheidt makes suggestions as to the use of the pedal, including the alto part played on a 4′ stop; and indicating that double-pedalling may be used for the tenor and bass parts, provided that the tenor does not go beyond c′.

Scheidt's *Modus ludendi* in six parts is worth practising at this stage for control of legato and melodic phrasing. It makes an excellent introduction to the more extended examples to be found in Louis Marchand (1669–1732) and J. S. Bach.

Next, the student should be introduced to the chorale preludes of Buxtehude. Many are short and simple in texture, but these highly expressive pieces will give further practice in the use of the pedals, both in the role of mainly harmonic support, and as independent melodic bass lines. The chorale melody is in the soprano part and may be played on a Cornet or a reed of the Krummhorn type.

Seven
The Baroque I

The French School

The French baroque organ school was initiated by Jean Titelouze, whose music derives from Renaissance style. It is essentially vocal, but with typical early baroque instrumentalizations in the final versets. His organ at Rouen was almost certainly influenced by the Flemish school, and his tonal world is that of the *plein jeu*, large and small – in other words, a mixture chorus on the Great and Chair Organs, capable of both richness and clarity in part-playing, the pedals giving a strong solo line to the cantus firmus. The Tierce was the only non-Flemish stop, and gave the reediness and plangency that was to become so marked a feature of French organ sonority. Titelouze's music does not need the Tierce for solo colours, but it was doubtless used in the full chorus for the final versets of his hymns and Magnificats.

The *plein jeu*, often based on a plainchant cantus firmus, was to remain a common feature of many organ masses and suites throughout the baroque period in France; along with contrasting short movements, with varying textures and colours, all based on standardized registrations characteristic of the French organ. Opera and dance greatly influenced style: textures included trios, with and without pedals, duos, and solo pieces such as *Basse de Trompette, Cromorne en Taille, Récit de Nasard* and *Tierce en Taille*. Rarely in the history of organ music has instrument and composition been so completely interdependent as in these

55

works, where the character of the music is implicit in the direction for registration used as the title for the movement.

Some of this music is variable in quality in comparison with contemporary German composition, but much is worthy of the greatest attention, as for instance, the two masses of François Couperin, the mass and hymns of Nicolas de Grigny, and the two suites on the first and second tones by Louis Nicolas Clérambault (1676–1749). Other collections well worth playing are *Livre d'orgue* by Pierre du Mage (1676–1751), *Premier livre de pièces d'orgue* by Jean Dandrieu (1682–1738), *Nouveau livre de Noëls* by Louis Claude Daquin (1694–1772) and selected pieces by Louis Marchand.

The organ at St Gervais in Paris, which Couperin would have played regularly, is fully representative of a mid-seventeenth-century Parisian instrument with four manuals. The *Grand Orgue* and the *Positif* obviously have their counterparts in the contemporary German *Werkprinzip* instruments. In addition large Parisian organs would have two short-compass manuals, the *Echo* and the *Récit*, this last keyboard usually restricted to a separate Cornet chest, for right-hand solo purposes. By comparison with the *Werkprinzip* the Pedal division shows no difference in character and function from the organs of the beginning of the century, a reed 8′ for the cantus firmus, and Flutes 8′ and 4′ for clear harmonic support and independent enough for simple trio textures.

Some of the most elegant and polished writing of the school is to be found in the Couperin masses and certain movements are ideal for introducing to the student at this point. The *Kyrie* from the *Messe pour les Paroisses* has five movements intended to be heard in alternation with the plainchant. The first and last sections are *plein jeu* cantus firmus movements and I would teach these first as a natural follow on from the Titelouze versets.

Both *plein jeu* movements would be played on the

ST GERVAIS, PARIS

Positif			Grand Orgue	
Bourdon	8		Montre	16
Montre	4		Bourdon	16
Flûte	4		Montre	8
Doublette	2		Bourdon	8
Fourniture	III		Prestant	4
Cymbale	III		Doublette	2
Nasard	2⅔		Fourniture	III
Tierce	1⅗		Cymbale	III
Larigot	1⅓		Flûte	4
Cromorne	8		Grosse Tierce	3⅕
			Nasard	2⅔
Echo			Tierce	1⅗
Bourdon	8		Trompette	8
Flûte	4		Clairon	4
Cymbale	III		Voix Humaine	8
Nasard	2⅔		Cornet	V
Doublette	2			
Tierce	1⅗		Récit	
Cromorne	8		Cornet Séparé	V
Pédale			Couplers: GO/Pos	
Flûte	8		GO/Péd	
Flûte	4			
Trompette	8		Tremblant doux, Tremblant fort	

coupled *Grand Orgue* and *Positif*, with foundation stops to Cymbale on both manuals. In the first *plein jeu* the cantus is played in the tenor register by the reed and Flute 8'; in the other it is played in the bass with all three pedal stops coupled to the *Grand Orgue*. These movements are much simpler in texture than Titelouze ones, but the same broad singing style is needed.

Two further movements from the Couperin *Messe* will make excellent study material, especially with regard to rhythmical treatment, at this stage. First, the *Benedictus*. This beautiful movement has the Cromorne en Taille (tenor register) accompanied by the *jeux doux* (Flutes 8', 4', possibly 16' if coupled to the Pedal Flute 8'). There is no finer piece for learning how to make a reed stop sing, with good phrasing and deliberate and expressive ornamentation. With this movement I would pair the fourth couplet from the *Gloria* versets. This uses a Trompette in dialogue between treble and bass, against a balanced *jeux*, based on a Bourdon 8′ and including stops up to Larigot 1⅓′.

These two movements are ideal for studying the application of rhythmical alteration known as *notes inégales*. In his harpsichord tutor *L'Art de toucher le clavecin*, Couperin explains, 'The Italians write their music in its true time values, but we do not. They play a diatonic succession of quavers evenly, whereas we always make the first of each pair a little longer than the second.' Obviously, the precise difference in value between notes played unequally will depend on the tempo and the character of the piece.

In the *Benedictus* the quavers may approximate to gentle triplets, making the first note slightly longer than the second:

In the *Gloria* the alteration of values should be more like:

, or even:

These two movements demonstrate extremes of *notes inégales*, but, as Couperin makes clear, the alteration should depend on the character of the pieces and the performer's own feeling for what is appropriate treatment. The precise rhythmical interpretation will depend on the character of the music and on the context in which they occur –

but usually means something like

and , or

When deciding whether to begin ornaments on the main or upper note, the note dissonant with the harmony should be chosen in every case. This often means the upper note but, as is often the case with Buxtehude and Couperin, it frequently means the main, when this is itself an appoggiatura.

Buxtehude: Wär Gott nicht mit uns diese Zeit

Couperin: Benedictus (Messe pour les Paroisses)

The *Elévation* from the *Messe pour les Convents* is a companion piece to the *Benedictus* in mood or 'affection'. It is marked *Tierce en Taille* and here in the tenor register what is required is a *Positif jeux* of 8.4.4.2⅔.1⅗.1⅓ – a compound registration of great richness, capable of more ease and flexibility than the Cromorne. This is recognized in the much more supple movement Couperin gives to this solo line, in comparison with the more restrained range and style of the solo line in the *Benedictus*. The accompanying *jeu doux* can certainly take 16′, 8′ and 4′ Flutes coupled to the 8′ Pedal.

The Couperin pieces might be followed by the *Suite du*

deuxième ton by Clérambault. This begins normally with a *plein jeu* movement with sections indicated for the *Grand* and *Positif Orgues*. The music for each manual is individually characterized: broad, chordal textures for the *Grand Orgue*, replete with expressive appoggiaturas, and enlivened by short flourishes in the French overture style; contrasted with more animated sections, marked *gay*, to be played on the *Positif*. Nowhere in the history of organ music is the thought and the sonority more closely interwoven.

Some alteration of note values is appropriate in both sections. The upbeat flourishes may be shortened and *notes inégales* may be applied both to the broad *Grand Orgue* passages, as well as the spirited *gay* ones, marked for the *Positif*. The second movement is a *Duo* in a lively dance idiom, again marked *gay*. Although in two-part texture, the character of the piece is strong and a *forte* registration is required, such as:

Right-hand *Positif*: 8.4.4.2⅔.1⅗.1⅓
Grand Orgue: 16.8.4.3⅕.2⅔.2

This *jeux* gives weight and richness to the texture, as well as clarity and brilliance.

The following *Trio* has two closely spaced upper parts in the manner of the Italian trio sonata, and a bass part of a highly melodic character. The upper voices may be given to the *Positif* Cromorne, perhaps with Flutes 8′ (or 4′) to fill out the tone if it is thin in the upper register; and the bass line needs the fullness of the Basse de Tierce 16.8.4.3⅕.5⅓.2⅔. This bass registration will give harmonic support and independence of line which would have supplied by the continuo of cello and harpsichord.

Next is a *Basse de Cromorne*, in which an 8′ Flute and a 4′ Principal should be added to fill out the solo line. The *jeux doux* would consist of Flutes 8′ and 4′. The lively character, together with the use of broken-chord figurations, makes the use of *notes inégales* inappropriate here.

The next movement, *Flûtes*, requires flute tone on three manuals: *Grand*, *Positif* and *Récit* (or *Echo*), and the *Récit de Nazard* which follows would be played on *Positif* 8', 4' and 2⅔' with *Grand Orgue* Flutes 8' and 4'. It is clear that Clérambault intended the use of the *Grand Orgue/Pédale* coupler in the last bar.

The last movement, *Caprice sur les grands jeux*, uses a registration dominated by reed tone. Trompette and Clairon 8' and 4', Cornets, Tierces and Principal 4' give a fierce and brilliant clangour, as effective in chordal textures highly spiced with dissonances as in fast fugal textures. The pedal Trompette 8' needs to be coupled to the *Grand Orgue* on the last page.

The French seventeenth-century organ was a very different instrument from that of the contemporary German school. It was very much an instrument of sharply contrasting colours, and in this respect it was a more truly baroque instrument than its German counterpart. The *plein jeux* was derived from the medieval *Blockwerk*, as was the German *organo pleno*, but whereas the German chorus, coloured by the lightly voiced reeds, was well suited to polyphony, the French preferred to separate the mixture chorus from the reeds and also favoured a more richly harmonic texture for the *plein jeux*. The *grands jeux* was reserved for dialogue movements, or for fugues. Admittedly, these were of no great length: aggressive reeds of the French type would quickly pall in lengthy, fully developed fugues on the German model. But while the separation of the *plein jeux* and *grands jeux* is such a crucial aspect of the French classical school it was the combination of these two choruses in the nineteenth-century organ that was to create the unique chorus of the French romantic instruments under the inspiration of Aristide Cavaillé-Coll.

The English School

Interest in the organ in England during the seventeenth century was desultory. The organ was still regarded as an accompanimental instrument, and its location on the choir screen in cathedrals ensured that it would remain an instrument of a relatively small size and limited function. The seventeenth-century English 'Double Organ' was fairly standardized by the middle of the century. The Robert Dallam instrument of 1632 in York Minster is typical.

YORK MINSTER

Great Organ		Chair Organ	
Open Diapason	8	Diapason	8
Open Diapason	8	Principal	4
Stopped Diapason	8	Flute	4
Principal	4	Small Principal	2
Principal	4	Recorder	2?
Twelfth	2⅔		
Small Principal	2		
Recorder	2		

The duplication of Open Diapasons 8' and Principals 4' in the Great Organ was presumably for ranks facing both east and west. Noticeable is the absence of a full mixture chorus based on 16' ranks, and an absence of reeds and colouristic solo stops such as the Tierce. It is an organ for the accompaniment of the Anglican choral service and for the performance of voluntaries and verses based on polyphonic vocal models: the fancies of Orlando Gibbons and the voluntaries of Thomas Weelkes (c.1575–1623) and Thomas Tomkins (1572–1656).

However, by 1661 Robert Dallam was designing a comprehensive organ in the French style of two manuals (but no pedals) and twenty-four stops, including the usual Fourniture and Cymbale, for New College, Oxford. The most interesting specification of this period is Bernard Smith's Chapel Royal organ of 1699, in which French and German influences are present in such a synthesis as to suggest its position as the first English eclectic organ.

CHAPEL ROYAL, WHITEHALL

Great Organ GGAA–c'''		Choir Organ GGAA–c'''	
Open Diapason	8	Stopped Diapason	8
Stopped Diapason	8	Principal	4
Principal	4	Flute	2?
Flute	4	Vox Humana	8
Block Flute	4	Cremona	8
Twelfth	2⅔		
Fifteenth	2	*Echo*	
Sesquialtera	III	*ga–c'''*	
Cornet	III	Open Diapason	8
Trumpet	8	Principal	4
		Cornet (12.17)	II
		Trumpet	8

The student can find useful preparation for the more extended pieces of this period in the seven organ voluntaries from *Melothesia* of 1673 by Matthew Locke (*c.*1630–1677). These short pieces would follow on well from Buxtehude's chorale preludes and lead to the organ works of Blow and Henry Purcell (1659–1695). The Voluntaries in A and G by Blow are certainly worth study, but they are surpassed in elegance and power by Purcell's Voluntary in G and his Voluntary for Double Organ. The G major is very Italianate in style. The opening slow section is rhapsodic and strongly reminiscent of the Frescobaldi toccata idiom – it might well be marked 'drag' – and this leads into a 'brisk' canzona-like fugal section. The Voluntary for Double Organ brings together Italian and French influences in a most convincing synthesis. The liberal use of ornaments, and the sweeping passages for the Great Organ in both hands suggest a French *dialogue* movement, but the piece is unified throughout by the use of short ritornello passages in canzona style. The many flourishes need a brilliant touch and a sense of fiery bravura, while still securely embedded in a solid basic pulse.

Eight
The Baroque II

J. S. Bach and the German Tradition

In his *Music in the Baroque Era* M. F. Bukofzer heads his
chapter on Bach: 'Fusion of National Styles'. This fusion
was as characteristic of the organs Bach is known to have
played and appreciated as of the music he wrote for them.
Among the composers whose work Bach knew well were
Frescobaldi (*Fiori musicale*), Buxtehude (chorale preludes, and preludes and fugues) and de Grigny (*Premier
livre d'orgue*).

Bach certainly knew the standard German *Werkprinzip*
instrument as exemplified in Buxtehude's organ at Lübeck
and the Arp Schnitger instrument at the Jakobikirche at
Hamburg, but the typical Thuringian organ was that of the
Neue Kirche, Arnstadt, built by J. F. Wender in 1699 and
1703. Here the tradition was not for Chair Organs and
pedal-towers, with carefully balanced choruses. The Pedal
of five stops was supportive rather than independent and
the *Brustwerk* would not have produced the penetrative
tone to match and complement the *Hauptwerk*.

Bach witnessed great changes in ideas about registration
in the first half of the eighteenth century. An organist of
Buxtehude's generation, with the *Werkprinzip* instrument,
would not have duplicated pitches with different families of
stops. According to Andreas Werckmeister this was because the stops did not blend, having a very pronounced
tonal characteristic, and because the winding did not allow
of such duplication. Only twenty years later, organists

64

were using complete flue choruses, Principals, Flutes and strings for the *plenum*; instead of a Cornet or Krummhorn, solo lines were thickened with the use of flues 8.8.4.4.4 and reeds 8′ and 8′.

Gottfried Silbermann's organs used an *Oberwerk* (placed.above the *Hauptwerk*) instead of a Chair Organ, and often very small Pedal divisions. The organ at Fraureuth exhibits the typical Silbermann blend of central German and French elements. The relationship of this instrument to the *Werkprinzip* and the Parisian classical organ, with special reference to the Pedal, should be considered. It was built between 1739 and 1742. Bach's interest in the French school may have endeared Silbermann's instruments to him, and it could be that his unusual registrations (apparently a source of surprise to his contemporaries) were derived from his knowledge of French practices.

Up to his arrival in Weimar, Bach's tonal world would generally have been that of the seventeenth-century German *Werkprinzip* or modifications of it. At Weimar and after he more often played instruments of the southern

FRAUREUTH

Hauptwerk		Oberwerk	
Prinzipal	8	Gedact	8
Rohrflöte	8	Rohrflöte	4
Quintadena	8	Nasat	2⅔
Oktave	4	Oktave	2
Spitzflöte	4	Quinte	1⅓
Quinte	2⅔	Sifflöte	1
Superoktave	2	Sesquialtera	1⅗
Tierce	1⅗	Zimbel	II
Mixtur	IV		
Cornet	III	*Pedal*	
		Subbass	16
Couplers: *Hw/Ob*		Posaune	16
Hw/Ped			
Tremulant			

Organ

Silbermann type. These were organs capable of a wide variety of colour, but characterized above all by beauty of tone, and highly suitable for music of a lyrical cast, with textures much influenced by Italianate string writing. However, it must be said that, in the opinion of C. P. E. Bach, his father never had the regular opportunity to play a really first-rate instrument.

Some Chorale Preludes

How should a student first approach Bach's organ music? Both from a technical and a musical point of view it is desirable for him to begin with a careful selection of the chorale preludes. In fact these pieces take us to the heart of Bach's music written for any medium. As was the composer's intention, the *Orgelbüchlein* provides a most useful set of pieces for teaching purposes. Some are of the right degree of difficulty to follow on naturally from the examples by Buxtehude: *Liebster Jesu* is an obvious choice. The part-writing is not much harder than that of a fairly elaborate chorale harmonization, but the canonic structure highlights the importance of the clear phrasing of two melodic lines played by the same hand.

Bach's title page makes it clear that he was writing for the beginner, and that the provision of material for pedal practice was one of his primary aims. Certainly the pedal parts in these preludes are as important as any other voice in the texture, and the feet are worked quite as hard as the hands. This equality of treatment was to lead to the composition of some of the most difficult organ pieces ever written: the Toccata in F (BWV 540), the Fugue in G minor (BWV 542), the last movement of Sonata No. 6 in G (BWV 530) – pieces in which the pedals are offered little or no respite. This use of the pedals stems from the bass parts of the string music of the Italian baroque, which was to exert such a potent influence on Bach's organ writing generally.

How might *Liebster Jesu* be registered? Bach asks for

66

two manuals so that the right-hand canon stands out clearly. I suggest:

Right hand: Krumhorn 8'; Flutes 8' and 4'

Left hand: Flutes 8' and 4' (fuller toned?)

Pedal 16' and 8' coupled to the left hand should balance well.

This prelude might be followed by *Ich ruf' zu dir* (BWV 639). The trio texture of this most expressive piece points both to the importance of phrasing, and to the influence of string technique. The repeated pedal notes suggest the accentuation of string basses:

and the left-hand semiquavers have a rare example of indicated phrasing:

This is string bowing, and it needs to have the smoothness and subtlety of good bow changes, rather than the mechanical gawkiness that comes so readily to keyboard players when confronted with this kind of phrasing mark.

Here we have a perfect miniature of organ music, absolutely idiomatic, yet it could easily be a transcription of a movement for oboe, viola obbligato and basso continuo, a useful reminder that Bach's organ writing tends to be less 'pure' than that of his seventeenth-century predecessors. We shall increasingly see that the organ works of the Weimar period and after derive much of their idiomatic style from Bach's knowledge of instrumental music of the Italian school.

One further example to demonstrate the immense variety of mood encompassed by this unique collection: the Christmas prelude *Christum wir sollen loben schon* (BWV 611). This fifteen-bar-long prelude has an immensity that matches the chorale text: 'From East to West, from shore to shore, let every heart awake and sing. . . .'

Organ

The chorale melody is a metricized version of the medieval plainsong tune, and Bach's treatment here evokes the ambience of a French *hymne* movement using the *plein jeux* by Titelouze or de Grigny. In fact the *plein jeux* colour seems absolutely right for it, except that the cantus firmus, in a more decorated form than the French would have used, is in the alto part, the pedal being needed for its own magnificent line, with its superb sweep and momentum, leading in the last two bars to the use of double-pedalling in order to maintain the richness of texture when the chorale reaches an internal pedal point. A full legato is required for this vocal polyphony, with breathing places as shown in my example.

If Bach saw the usefulness of the *Orgelbüchlein* for teaching beginners – and it certainly would be impossible to find a better introduction to his work under one cover – we may find some of the miscellaneous preludes even more appealing for some students. They tend to be overlooked

Adagio — Bach: Christum wir sollen loben scho (BWV 611)

in favour of the great collections, but though there are some immature works they do contain pieces as fine as any.

Herzlich tut mich verlangen (BWV 727), surprisingly Bach's only organ prelude on the Passion chorale, is slightly easier than the *Orgelbüchlein* pieces, yet its heart-felt magic will endear it to any student, young or old. It is a perfect example of the coloratura type of prelude much cultivated by Georg Böhm (1661–1733) after the example of Buxtehude and the French solo movements of their suites and masses. In this prelude the melody is virtually

68

unaltered; only the cadences are delicately 'coloured'. As with *Ich ruf' zu dir*, the melody might effectively be given to the Cornet or Sesquialtera, with the accompanying parts played on Flutes 8' and 4'.

A striking instance of Bach's rare use of double-pedalling is to be found in *Wir glauben all' an einen Gott, Vater* (BWV 740). This is reminiscent of Scheidt's use of tenor and bass parts played on the pedal, and the occasional use of the device by the French classical composers. It makes a very worthwhile and delightful study, requiring much work on the pedal parts alone to ensure perfect control of phrasing, before adding the two-manual accompanying voices, and finally the chorale phrases. An 8' Principal would suit the pedal parts well, with a characterful 8' Flute for the manuals. Flutes 8' and 4' with the Tierce would do well for the chorale melody.

Some Large-scale Works

How best can the student be introduced to Bach's large-scale works? It seems logical to begin not only with pieces that are of the right technical standard, but also with those that are not too extended, and, perhaps most important, those in which Bach's development from the work of his predecessors can be traced. I would choose the E minor Prelude and Fugue (BWV 533), which is very reminiscent of Buxtehude, and then a group of Italianate works: the *Alla breve* (BWV 589), the *Fugue on a Theme of Corelli* BWV 579) and the Canzona in D minor (BWV 588), a fully developed study of the Frescobaldi canzona, and finally the Fantasia in G.

The Fantasia in G (BWV 572)
The G major Fantasia is an extraordinary conception. At the centre of the work is a huge *plein jeux* movement, marked *gravemente*. It is as if Bach had taken the opening of Couperin's *Messe pour les Convents* and set out to show just what an extended piece could be developed with such

material. This massive piece of five-part polyphony is framed with a sparkling and exuberant *très vitement* section for manuals alone, somewhat resembling a keyboard version of a solo violin movement, a marvellous example of Bachian single-voice harmony, and closes with two pages of toccata-like writing, this time with pedal. It is a startlingly original scheme and convincingly demonstrates, at this (presumably) early stage in Bach's career, just how the Italian, French and German styles might be fused into a triumphant stylistic unity.

This fascinating work poses some interesting registrational problems. Obviously the *gravemente* needs the French *plein jeux*: 16' to the Cymbal with a chorus to balance on the Pedal, coupled to the Great if necessary. If we couple the Great and Positive mixture choruses together, as we should for the *plein jeux*, then we can conveniently begin on the Positive for the *très vitement*. This will give us the unity of tone so desirable, as this opening section runs into the *gravemente* with the minimum of break. Bach is clearly determined to emphasize the unity of his unusual formal scheme, and ends the *gravemente* on a dramatic interrupted cadence, with a diminished seventh.

The final section (*lentemente*) takes us away from the diminished seventh chord by descending chromatic steps in the bass to a final cadential flourish. It would here be appropriate to add to the *plein jeux* Cornets, Tierces and reeds 8' and 4' on the manuals and reeds (32'), 16' and 8' on the Pedal, thus providing a German integration of *plein jeux* and *grand jeux*.

Technique and Phrasing: The Trio Sonatas

After the intoxicating sonorities and textures of the Fantasia, Bachian studies will need something to develop technique along rigorous lines, with less emphasis on sheer sound. One of the trio sonatas would be ideal.

It seems likely that, as with the *Orgelbüchlein*, Bach

wished to provide his students with a comprehensive course of 'finishing' material, possibly with his son Wilhelm Friedemann (1710–1784) in mind. Trio textures were already common in organ music, but the examples in the French school rarely involved pedals. The six sonatas are one more example of a unique genre the composer invented from a mere hint in the previous work of other men, and took to an unrepeatable and triumphant conclusion. These sonatas are unsurpassed, both as music and as technical material for study.

They sound at their best on a moderately sized two-manual and Pedal Organ in a not too resonant room. Obviously the manual and Pedal choruses need to be well balanced, but it is worth making the point that the solo and tutti spatial arrangement of the seventeenth-century *Werkprinzip* organ, with its strongly characterized personalities of *Rückpositiv* and *Hauptwerk*, may not be the most appropriate instrument on which to play these sonatas with their closely integrated lines and textures. The mid-eighteenth-century Silbermann type, with a *Brustwerk* or *Oberwerk*, is probably the better instrument to use. In considering registration, clarity and balance must be the main concern. Here is one possible scheme:

1 Left hand: Flute 8′; Principal 4′
   Right hand: Flutes 8′ and 4′; Octave 2′
   Pedal Subbass 16′; Principal 8′; Flute 4′
2 Contrasting Flutes 8′ on manuals and pedal
3 Left hand: Flute 8′; Octave 4′; Superoctave 2′
   Right hand: Gedact 8′; Rohrflöte 4′; Quinte 1⅓′ (Sifflöte 1′)
   Pedal Subbass 16′; Principal 8′; Octave 4′

The First Sonata is possibly the most straightforward and is certainly one of the most attractive, a good first choice for study. The Italian trio sonata was Bach's model for these pieces, and even if we cannot identify any of the movements of this sonata as being transcriptions of instrumental pieces, as is the case with several of the other sonatas, at least both the first and second movements sound like string or wind and string pieces. The first movement might be a sonata da camera (or even a double violin concerto), whereas in the second we hear a flute and violin with basso continuo in the rhythm of a celestial Siciliana.

In the outer movements a robust sound approximating to the eighteenth-century concerto orchestra seems appropriate for these vigorous pieces; the middle movement is best treated as a trio of solo voices. There are parallels for this in the concertos of Bach. When we consider phrasing we are bound at once to think of string bowing techniques, for instance,

Notated symbols cannot show the subtlety of touch required. If the organist cannot play baroque music on the violin (as Bach could), then he needs to listen closely to good performances on authentic instruments, or try these sonatas on a pedal harpsichord in order to begin to understand the delicacy of approach required.

It is not without significance that a good deal of baroque keyboard music can be transferred from organ to harpsichord or clavichord with equally convincing results. It was just as appropriate for Liszt to provide arrangements for the late nineteenth-century piano of his organ works. We may want (and need) to play Bach and Liszt on the same organ, but we need to analyse the difference between the harpsichord and the nineteenth-century piano if we are to begin to approach the two periods of music stylistically.

Now we can look at the second movement:

Here again, the articulation and phrasing of a good flute- or string-player should be our model. The second section begins with an inversion of the opening material. This can sound very dull unless we apply the ornamentation implicit at the beginning. Obviously we shall need to give as much attention to the consistent phrasing of the pedal (cello) part as of the manual voices.

When we come to the last movement, a lively binary piece, we seem to be in the world of the keyboard partitas:

yet here also string technique seems to lie behind the music's motives and their development. After all, interchangeability of instrumental and vocal idioms is one of the hallmarks of the baroque period.

Contrast and Continuity: The Preludes and Fugues

So far we have noticed the use of different manuals and changes of registration in trio textures; between variations; dialogue and echo effects, as in Sweelinck and the French school; and solo and accompaniment textures, as in a *Tierce en Taille* movement or a chorale prelude.

We now need to consider the possible use of manual changes within a movement, where no guidance is given by the composer. The only manual changes indicated almost certainly by Bach himself are in his concerto arrangements and the Dorian Toccata (BWV 538); in both cases the indications are for *Oberwerk* (Great Organ) and *Rückpositiv* (Chair Organ). The contrast between solo and tutti in a concerto design would appear to lie behind these indications, but what about works in which the concerto structure is less explicit?

In the E minor Prelude and Fugue (BWV 548), for instance, both movements appear to have a concerto-like approach – ought we to attempt to bring this out with appropriate manual changes? The Prelude is in a clear ritornello form – can we play the episodes on a second manual? The answer, provided by a thoughtful scrutiny of the texture, appears to be no. As so often in his mature work, Bach seems to be intent on maximum continuity, and he obtains contrast of texture by omitting the pedals in many of the episodic passages. However much the piece is indebted to concerto style, dynamic contrasts of solo and tutti are not part of the intended scheme here.

The Fugue is another immense ritornello design; it is not a da capo or ternary fugue (a reasonable description of BWV 537). Bach merely repeats the opening ritornello (fugal exposition) complete at the end, as he does in so many of his preludial movements. The difference here is simply one of scale. In a fugue of such gigantic proportions it was perfectly natural for Bach to repeat the opening ritornello in its entirety, which is certainly his normal procedure in concerto movements. After all, the structural connection between the fugue and the ritornello form is clear for all to see, and here Bach once again triumphantly unites the two forms. But in spite of its very clear solo/tutti structure, are we justified in changing manuals in this fugue of long episodes and frequent appearances of the ritornello material? Yet again, the answer is no. Bach is concerned rather to let one idea or section grow out of another as smoothly as possible. Why break up this continuity of line and texture with unnecessary changes of tone colour?

The same is true of stop changes. There is neither opportunity nor musical justification for the addition or subtraction of stops. We might expect the climactic point in the Fugue which leads so explosively into the repeat of the opening exposition/ritornello to be recognized with the addition of a reed stop. But, no, again: all the tension is in the music and an increase of tone would be quite pointless.

So, if these two large-scale movements ought not to have changes made in the course of them, what tonal contrasts can be made between them? I suggest that both need a plenum of similar volume, but of differing quality. For the Prelude I suggest a mixture chorus based on 16' Principal tone, coloured with light reeds 16' and 8'. For the Fugue we can omit the reeds and 16' but add further mixture work. This movement can certainly take more brilliance and sparkle in the tone than the more darkly hued Prelude. The Pedal for both movements should be a mixture chorus, with 16' reed, possibly coupled to the manuals if a good balance or sufficient unity of tone is lacking.

Playing experience, or even a glance at the specification of many Schnitger and Silbermann organs, makes it clear that the Pedal divisions were not designed to balance the manuals in *forte* and *fortissimo*. The baroque-organ 'independent pedal at all costs' is a myth, and one that has been too readily accepted.

When we turn to another late Prelude and Fugue, the C major (BWV 545), we encounter two of the most seamless organ movements Bach ever wrote. Every fugue of Bach's tends to be of startling originality: here the pedal is silent for the opening forty-eight bars and then enters with the subject in augmentation. Is it not part of the architecture of this movement to change manuals or add stops at this point? Once again, the polished continuity of the part-writing makes changing musically unsatisfactory. In fact this mighty pedal entry makes the point clear: in Bach's textures, all the tonal contrast and variety he needs or expects is provided by the use or omission of the pedals. The only exceptions to this rule are works in clearly defined sections (usually early ones) such as the D major Prelude (BWV 532), and small-scale echo or answering effects, as in the 'Jig' Fugue or the Dorian Toccata.

We can now look at the E minor Prelude and Fugue (BWV 548) again with regard to points of style, phrasing and articulation. The opening idea of the Prelude immediately recalls string idioms as the basis of its inspiration. The opening phrase is as good an example of a keyboard realization of solo violin writing (with double-stopping) as is, in its very different way, the opening of the much earlier Fantasia in G (BWV 572). The tremendous sweep of this theme launches one of its composer's most tightly knit movements on its way. If we are to project its impetus, we need to get the rhetorical gesture of a solo string-player

Organ

Bach: Prelude and Fugue in E minor (BWV 548)
Prelude

into the gritty dissonances, as if we can feel the bow digging into the strings. The episodic motives might be articulated on these lines:

Once again, the more we can hear the sound of the violin in this music, the better we shall communicate it to the hearer.

The Fugue subject is a string-inspired theme, based on an imaginative use of a standard baroque progression. The single-line writing in much of the episodic work is not thin, but explicable as string/keyboard writing, needing no tonal change; all the contrast needed is there in the texture.

Fugue

The influence of Italian string writing is so apparent in the concerto transcriptions, and such pieces as the Schübler chorale preludes, that we are apt to forget its overriding importance for the understanding of the right way to play Bach's organ music in general. Perhaps the idioms of the solo string instrument and that of the multi-keyboard wind giant seem to be opposed but I hope that I have demonstrated that this is not so.

76

It should be evident from this discussion that to begin to comprehend Bach's organ music we need to know well:

The evolution of organ music before Bach;

Bach's special interest in the music of his predecessors;

His music for other media;

The development of his style in the context of the changing tastes of the period;

The developments in organ design during Bach's working life.

Bach provides a logical centrepoint in a consideration of the art of the organ and its music. He remains the central figure, not only of the baroque era, but also of the evolution of the instrument and its music in Western civilization, from the medieval period onwards.

After Bach's death in 1750, Man rather than God as the subject of mankind's proper study assumed an ever-increasing importance. If the organ is the supreme God-instrument, it should come as no surprise that the organ and its repertoire declined in importance as fast as Man's idea of God. Bach himself, the God-intoxicated composer, was wellnigh forgotten.

Nine

English Organ Music 1700–1800

Before we leave the baroque period we must consider a relatively minor, though charming, backwater. We noticed, in discussing the voluntaries of Locke, Blow and Purcell, the importance of Italian and French influences in England, first on the music, and later on the organs. French influence increased during the eighteenth century, although the English Diapason chorus never included a plenum of 16′ to mixture, as did the French *plein jeux*.

The English organ remained a comparatively mild affair, without Pedal divisons. The Harris and Byfield organ of 1726 at St Mary Redcliffe, Bristol, had one octave of pedal pulldowns, a new feature in England, and a manual coupler of some kind. The available reeds and mutations must have made this one of the most French-sounding organs in England. Even if it could not manage a *plein jeux*, it surely could have given a good account of a *Dialogue sur les grands jeux* such as the last movement of Clérambault's *Suite du premier ton*. English organ music of the eighteenth century, though, was to turn away from the excitable and colourful French school, in the direction of the more mellifluous Italian style, firmly led by George Frideric Handel (1685–1759).

The swell box, claimed to be new in 1712 by Abraham Jordan, had become standard by about 1830. Putting the shutters of the echo-box under the foot control of the player was an obvious piece of technical innovation – its advantage for varied balances, as opposed to 'swelling' the tone, is evident. However, the St Mary Redcliffe Echo was

ST MARY REDCLIFFE, BRISTOL

Great Organ		Chair Organ	
CC–d''' (63 notes)		GG–d''' (56 notes)	
Open Diapason	8	Stopped Diapason	8
Open Diapason	8	Principal	4
Stopped Diapason	8	Flute Almain	4?
Principal	4	Flute	2?
Twelfth (from GG)	2⅔	Sesquialtera	III
Fifteenth (from GG)	2	Bassoon	8
Tierce (from G)	1⅗		
Sesquialtera	V	*Swell*	
Cornet (from c')	V	G–d''' (44 notes)	
Trumpet	8	Open Diapason	8
Clarion	4	Stopped Diapason	8
		Principal	4
Pedal		Flute	4
1 octave pulldowns		Cornet (complete)	III
Octave coupler on *Great*?		Trumpet	8
		Hautboy	8
		Cremona	8
		French Horn	8

'made to swell or express Passion', so the confusion between a mere mechanical increase of tone, compared with the genuine intensity of crescendo obtainable on string or wind instruments, was apparent from the earliest appearances of this new invention.

The English eighteenth-century composers concentrated almost exclusively on the fugue and voluntary; there is no liturgical basis to the music as in the case of the German chorale prelude and the French *hymne* and Mass versets. This absence of an accepted function in the Anglican Service is the most potent reason for the comparative insignificance of both quantity and quality of the music.

In France and Germany the pedals developed independently from the manuals, as carriers of a plainchant cantus firmus or a chorale melody. Undoubtedly the absence of this function in English organ music is the fundamental reason for the tardy appearance of Pedal departments in England. As for the liturgical use of voluntaries, the most common practice was to insert one after the Psalms, and another at the close of the service. They were intended as pleasing interludes or postludes, having no essential connection with the liturgy.

The increasing Frenchification of the English organ at the end of the seventeenth century allowed for an emphasis on tone colour as a leading characteristic of each voluntary. A favourite plan was a two-movement design, consisting of a slow introduction on a Diapason chorus 8' and 4' (+?2') *mezzo-forte* or *forte* leading into a fast Cornet or Trumpet tune. It was common enough for the trumpet to be imitated in seventeenth-century harpsichord music, and the new Trumpet stop on English organs was ripe for exploitation in far lengthier movements. The slow–fast structure was ideal for leading congregations into a secular gaiety of mood by means of a restrained and sober adagio.

The idiom of the harpsichord and the trumpet played their part, but more substantial pieces were written, reminiscent of the French overture, with a slow introduction in dotted rhythm and a fugal allegro, and even three-movement concertos in the Vivaldi idiom, with the Chair Organ responsible for the episodes in true continental style.

Handel

The development of the voluntary owes most to the influence of Handel – naturally enough, as he dominated English music throughout the eighteenth century. His most important contribution was in the organ concerto – a genre which he virtually invented and made his own. His Six Fugues, Op. 3, (1735) are strong pieces, the equivalent of the fugal movements in the concerti grossi or the oratorios. Principal choruses of appropriate dynamic levels, according to the character of each fugue, suit them best, with no stop changes. But in the posthumously published voluntaries we see him establishing the two-movement form, with the registrations, either Cornet, Trumpet or Full Organ, clearly indicated.

The concertos are best played on a chamber organ – one manual is all that is needed for these slender textures, so like harpsichord style. Apart from cadential ornamentation, Handel does not require thickening of his textures. Many editions have been made, incorporating pedal parts and lavish filling out of the harmonic texture. All, though, are superfluous. Handel wrote one concerto with a pedal part (Second Set, No. 7), and he occasionally asks for a short improvised movement to link two substantial allegros. Apart from this only a little judicious continuo-style harmonic filling is needed in the more homophonic movements.

These concerti are essentially chamber music, and the use of a chamber organ is strongly recommended, whatever conductors may say about expense and audience preference for the 'grand style'. The necessary intimate integration of solo part with orchestra (ideally, perhaps, directed by the soloist) is impossible in an inflated performance with large organ and orchestra widely separated.

The sets of voluntaries by Boyce, Maurice Greene (1695–1755) and John Travers (c.1703–1758) are all worth study, but the most charming and polished examples are probably those by John Stanley. Certainly unpretentious and slight in comparison with the German and French schools, this music nevertheless has something vital to say. The voluntaries fit well at this point of the student's curriculum as a lightener to the more extended works of the German school and they are the best material to lead on to a study of the Handel concertos. In their elegance and lightness of touch they will develop those same qualities in the student's playing.

Ten
Interlude: The Classical Decline
1750–1850

Pleasing though the English eighteenth-century school is, it does serve to illustrate something of an impending decadence in the art of the organ. The voluntary was entertainment music, divorced from any liturgical requirement, and this attitude to the instrument and its music was not confined to England. The increasing affluence of both the Church and the town councils, together with the growing desire to exploit new technology in the service of expansion of resources, meant that organs were now ripe for development, although what form it might take was, as yet, uncertain. And this was the very time that organ composition was undergoing its sharp decline from the peak it had reached in the work of J. S. Bach.

Music as decoration; as the vehicle for *Sturm-und-Drang* expositions of individualism, or as the vehicle for the merely picturesque and the sensational, was unlikely to accord with the logical severity of the *Werkprinzip* ideal. Instead of clarity, a more fully saturated sound in the tutti became the trend, while at the other end of the spectrum extreme delicacy and an increasing range of imitative colours were sought after. Competition between town councils was an obvious factor in the new developments – but where were the composers to be inspired by the tonal resources?

A study of the organ of 1762–7 in the Michaeliskirche, Hamburg, reveals the emphasis on richness of tone, on blend, and on a wide variety of colouristic possibilities. One could certainly play the repertoire on this instrument,

MICHAELISKIRCHE, HAMBURG

Hauptwerk C–f‴		*Brustwerk*	
Prinzipal	16	C–f‴	
Quintadena	16	Rohrflöte	16
Oktave	8	Prinzipal	8
Gedackt	8	Flauto traverso	8
Gemshorn	8	Gedackt	8
Viola da gamba	8	Rohrflöte	8
Quinte	5⅓	Oktave	4
Oktave	4	Rohrflöte	4
Gemshorn	4	Nasat	2⅔
Nasat	2⅔	Oktave	2
Oktave	2	Tierce	1⅗
Sesquialtera	II	Quinte	1⅓
Mixtur	VIII(2)	Sifflöte	I
Scharf	V(1⅓)	Rauschpfeife	II–III
Cornet	V	Zimbel	V
Trompete	16	Chalumeau	8
Trompete	8		

Oberwerk C–f‴		*Pedal* C–d′	
Bourdon	16	Prinzipal	32
Prinzipal	8	Prinzipal	16
Spitzflöte	8	Subbass	32
Quintatön	8	Subbass	16
Unda maris	8	Rohrquinte	10⅔
Oktave	4	Oktave	8
Spitzflöte	4	Quinte	5⅓
Quinte	2⅔	Oktave	4
Oktave	2	Mixtur	X(2⅔)
Rauschpfeife	II	Posaune	32
Zimbel	V(1⅓)	Posaune	16
Echo Cornet (treble)	V	Fagott	16
Trompete	8	Trompete	8
Vox humana	8	Trompete	4

Tremulant for *Hw* (tremblant fort)	Four Ventils
Schwebung for *Ow* (tremblant doux)	Coupler: *Hw/Ped*
Zimbelstern	Manual shove-couplers

83

but it gives the impression of really being intended for some other function. The new homophonic orchestral style, with its strong contrasts of timbre and its operatically excited manner, must be an influence. For the first time in the history of the organ its basically calm and monumental nature and the demands of a new musical aesthetic were to come into severe conflict.

The Michaeliskirche instrument combines elements of the north German tradition with some Silbermann influences – the builder, J. G. Hildebrandt, was the son of a Silbermann pupil. But in its very completeness, with many duplications, it gives a somewhat overblown impression, as of a noble tradition going to seed. Charles Burney tells us that three (unspecified) stops were in a swell box, and he notes the lack of clarity in the sound: 'more striking by its force and the richness of the harmony, than by a clear and distinct melody'. An organ more suited to harmony than counterpoint is precisely the impression we get from an examination of its specification.

A perfect illustration of the impending decline of the instrument and its music is the fact that the three greatest composers of the classical period wrote a mere handful of organ pieces each, and all intended for the extremely popular, novelty 'clock' organs. The coincidence of the apparent culmination of the baroque organ with the disappearance of its repertoire was of no practical consequence to the classical musicians. Any involvement with the organ for them was in the framework of the Catholic liturgy in Austria, which allowed little scope for highly developed pieces.

Apart from the Epistle Sonatas of Wolfgang Amadeus Mozart (1756–1791), which had a liturgical function as an interlude between the Epistle and Gospel, there is nothing of significance by the Viennese masters intended for the extremely large organs that were becoming common all over Europe. However, we do need to consider the merits of the 'clock' pieces that these composers left us. The *32 Pieces* by Joseph Haydn (1732–1809) are mostly short and unpretentious but are certainly worth study for delicacy of touch and finesse of phrasing. But they pale into insignificance in comparison with the three extended works Mozart wrote, albeit with some reluctance, towards the end of his life.

Mozart

The Andante in F (K.616) follows on naturally from the Haydn pieces. Contrasting 8′ Flutes on two manuals is all that is needed to bring out the entrancing musical-box *naïveté* of this by no means easy piece. The two Fantasias in F minor (K.594) and (K.608) belong to the period when Mozart was exploring the riches of baroque polyphony and they provide the same fascinating amalgam of classical and baroque style to be found in the String Quartet in G (K.387) and the 'Jupiter' Symphony.

These Fantasias are best left until some of the larger preludes and fugues of Bach have been mastered. Much of the difficulty lies in the fact they were not intended for human hands and feet to contend with. Ideally they need a mechanical organist! It is not without significance that when Mozart came to transcribe these pieces for human hands he did them for piano duet rather than for organ solo.

Fantasia in F minor (K.608)
K.608 is perhaps the finest tribute we have to the late eighteenth-century organ. There appears to be no place for the *Werkprinzip Rückpositiv*; rather a tutti of richness and attack, with and without reeds for the opening and closing sections, and a variety of delicate orchestral colours for the variations, is required. Here in fact is the ideal piece for the Hamburg organ. The dilemma of the increasing magnificence of the instrument and its feeble contemporary repertoire is highlighted by the tragic grandeur of these Mozart works.

Eleven
The Romantic Revival: Germany

The organ in nineteenth-century Germany was increasingly dominated by influences from outside the Church. The first was the concentration on operatic and operatically based music, the sonata and the symphony. This led to a melodic virtuoso-based style of keyboard writing, and an orchestral idiom based on richness and homogeneity of sound, with wide dynamic contrasts. The organ could never expect to be able to imitate the flexibility of tone, accent and dynamics of the classical–romantic orchestra. Therefore it was left simply with the opaque richness of sound, which could no longer clarify counterpoint or provide the true baroque solo colours; nor could it match the electric excitement of the new orchestral style. Nevertheless, this was the impossible aim of such builders as Eberhard Friedrich Walcker in Germany and Cavaillé-Coll in France.

Inside the Church, the development of congregational singing, with a new 'romantic' repertoire of hymns, was thought to need a comparable warmth of accompaniment which might best be supplied with an increased number of 'blending' 8' stops. The shrill brilliance of the baroque mixture chorus was certainly at odds with the orchestral sound and the new lyrical approach that was now expected. The Tierce mixtures which were popular at the beginning of the century quickly began to pall; they were wearisome in accompaniment and unsuitable for contrapuntal textures. As a result mixtures in general fell from favour and this dislike was to last for a century or more.

There was also a growing internationalism in knowledge and taste. As the English and the French wanted to play Bach, many fine classical organs throughout Europe were rebuilt at the expense of their national characteristics – and usually of their natural tonal qualities. This ever-growing internationalism of taste, together with the ideal of the imitation romantic orchestra, and the cult of technological monumentalism, resulted in the organ being tempted into strange paths. After all, the nineteenth century was the century of unlimited material progress: why should the organ be exempt? It is therefore not surprising that the emergence of first-rate organ music was slow, and that when it did appear it was a direct outcome of the gradual revival of knowledge of Bach's organ music.

Mendelssohn

The leader in the rediscovery of Bach was Felix Mendelssohn (1809–1847). In his Three Preludes and Fugues (1835–7), and Six Sonatas (1844–5), he set entirely new standards in seriousness of approach and masterly workmanship in nineteenth-century organ composition.

The Sonatas were commissioned by the English publishers Coventry and Hollier in the form of voluntaries, and were assembled from twenty-four pieces written between 1844 and 1845. The First and Fourth Sonatas have a normal four-movement design, but the others are more loosely grouped sets of movements, and it could be that they were assembled as sonatas at a later stage, rather than 'thought through' from the outset.

Reminiscences of baroque forms are present in the use of chorale themes in the First, Third and Sixth Sonatas and even more so in the use of baroque structures, rather than classical sonata forms. The last movement of the Fifth Sonata is clearly based on the scheme used by Bach in his Prelude in C minor (BWV 546), but all the larger movements show baroque influence. The sonatas also contain movements in the characteristic idiom of the composer's

Songs without Words, but other movements, notably the finale of the First Sonata and the last variation on the chorale *Vater unser in Himmelreich* from the Sixth Sonata anticipate the French toccata style.

These Sonatas, then, are of crucial importance for many nineteenth-century developments. They suggest a neo-classical outlook; some use of the current contemporary style, and a looking forward to new and important developments. They are invaluable to the student. The slow movements are not difficult to play, yet offer excellent practice in phrasing, registration, and the subtle use of rubato.

As Mendelssohn was writing for England, it is quite reasonable to use the swell pedal, and an expressive approach generally appears to be intended by the composer. The use of stop addition and subtraction is equally legitimate, and it is probably true to say that these sonatas represent the first successful attempt to exploit the resources of the early nineteenth-century organ in the spirit of J. S. Bach.

It is important to give careful attention to Mendelssohn's phrasing indications. They are usually concerned with articulation within the structural phrasing, and recall classical bowing techniques. The fugue from the Second

Allegro moderato   Mendelssohn: Sonata No. 2 *Fuga*

Sonata is a good example. The phrasing does not indicate breathing places but the articulation necessary to give rhythmic point and vitality to the phrase. In their avoidance of phrasings across the beat or bar, Mendelssohn's indications are reminiscent of baroque idioms, and are a useful guide to organ phrasing generally. Where a sustained legato is required, as in the fugue from the Sixth Sonata, Mendelssohn leaves out phrasing altogether, taking the view that there is no need to indicate the obvious.

Although the shorter movements tend to the insubstantial and sentimental, there is much that is worthwhile in these Sonatas and they are essential material with which to lead the student from Bach to the romantic period.

Schumann

The year in which Mendelssohn's Sonatas appeared, 1845, was also the year in which Schumann's interest in Bach and in baroque polyphony was to result in some new and important work for the instrument. The diffidence with which the romantic school of composers approached the organ is well illustrated by the case of Robert Schumann (1810–1856).

Abandoning his first intention to study the organ, he approached the instrument through his favourite medium, the piano, writing three sets of pieces for pedal piano, an instrument that had just been introduced into the Leipzig Music School for the organ scholars' practice. Schumann had taught composition at the school since 1843 and it would seem that his imagination was quickly fired by the possibilities of the pedal attachment. The Schumanns hired one for their own piano and soon set to work on music conceived in pianistic terms, but very much influenced by Bachian counterpoint. The results show that Schumann did have the organ in mind, but his pianistic approach means that some adaptation is often necessary if the pieces are to sound well on the instrument.

The *Six Fugues on the Name of Bach*, Op. 60, are the most consistently contrapuntal in texture and fit relatively easily on to the organ. In the Six Studies, Op. 56, the composer concentrates on canon, and the idiom is much more pianistic, while the Four Sketches, Op. 58, are conceived too markedly in piano terms to fit easily on the organ. But they are such delightful music that the effort to find a good edition – or adapt one's own – is certainly worthwhile.

Organ

Schumann's approach to the organ through the piano was to be very influential, especially for the French school in the second half of the century. The influence of romantic pianism, for instance the use of staccato chordal writing in the Canon in B minor, was to exert no little influence on such composers as César Franck (1822–1890), Charles Marie Widor (1844–1937), Louis Vierne (1870–1937) and Marcel Dupré (1886–1971). This pianistic writing was also to lead to a demand for an organ action light enough to be comparable to the piano. From this movement all modifications of mechanical action, which had remained in essence unchanged from the medieval period, were to flow.

A selection of Schumann's pieces may follow the Mendelssohn Sonatas to good purpose. Of the Four Sketches, the Second and Third are the most useful and interesting, on both musical and technical grounds. The Fifth of the Canonic Studies is the most delightful, and introduces something new in organ textures, with its mainly staccato, chordal writing – though Mendelssohn had introduced staccato writing for the pedals in his works. With their sustained contrapuntal textures the Six Fugues fit very well on to the organ, the most original conception being the scherzo-like Fifth. The idea of a scherzo for organ was something new, and again it was the French school which was to take it up to good purpose.

The organ was now ripe to be translated to the concert hall, where its vastly increased size could rival the huge orchestra of Hector Berlioz (1803–1869) and Richard Wagner (1813–1883), and its new, pianistically based repertoire might rival the virtuosity of such keyboard lions as Frédéric Chopin (1810–1849) and Franz Liszt (1811–1886). From being *the* 'instrument' of the baroque it now became, in accordance with the monumental ideas of the age, the 'King of Instruments'.

From the student's point of view, attention now needs to move from a comparison with harpsichord touch to a comparison with piano touch. This is by no means an easy thing to do and it is the most obvious reason why some performers find it more congenial to specialize either in that area of the repertoire up to the end of the eighteenth century, or that beginning in the early nineteenth. Both want to play Bach of course. He is the point on which the whole corpus of organ music pivots.

Liszt

Liszt's organ music took the instrument a long way along the path towards the concert hall and virtuosity. Like Schumann, he worked at the pedal piano, but was sufficiently fascinated by the new style of organ to want to play it himself, usually exercising his talent for improvisation, to the delight of his friends.

His first important organ work was also his largest, the Fantasia and Fugue on the chorale *Ad nos, ad salutarem undam* from the opera *Le Prophète* (1859) by Giacomo Meyerbeer (1791–1864). In this work Liszt skilfully integrates the incongruous world of the Lutheran chorale with the excitement of the 'spectacle' opera of the early nineteenth century, rivalling the contemporary orchestra and piano in weight of tone and brilliance.

The other two important organ works, the *Prelude and Fugue on BACH* (1855) and the *Variations on Bach's 'Weinen, Klagen, Sorgen, Zagen'* (1863), also exist in piano versions, making clear the intimate connection between the two instruments in Liszt's mind. Both works take us back very firmly to Bach, though both are thoroughly modern – even avant-garde – in their use of a chromatic language unsurpassed in any other music of Liszt. For Humphrey Searle (*The Music of Liszt*) the *Prelude and Fugue on BACH* is a direct link between Bach and Schoenberg. Unlike the Schumann *Fugues on the Name of Bach*, Liszt's work is truly a fantasy, as of a romantic seeking to express the tumultuous feelings that the contemplation of Bach's art inspired in him. The fugal writing

91

Organ

is free and episodic, newly creative, rather than nostalgic or neo-classical.

The *Variations* on the Bach ground bass are less spectacular, but even more expressive, inspired as they were by the death of his daughter Blandine. The theme is taken from Bach's cantata of the same name, and Liszt concludes by quoting the chorale also used by Bach, *Was Gott tut, das ist wohlgetan* (What God does is well done). It is less formidable technically than either of the other two works and I would begin the exploration of the Lisztian organ world with this work; or if not with this then with a selection of the shorter pieces or transcriptions.

The specification of an organ Liszt would have known, for instance, the cathedral at Merseburg, is relevant at this point. The Merseburg organist, Alexander Winterberger

---

MERSEBURG CATHEDRAL

Hauptwerk		*Rückpositiv*	
Prinzipal	16	Prinzipal	8
Prinzipal	8	Bordun	16
Oktave	4	Flauto traverso	8
Spitzflöte	4	Gamba	8
Gedackt	4	Quintatön	8
Quinte	2⅔	Prinzipal	4
Oktave	2	Gedackt	4
Doublette	4–2	Oktave	2
Mixtur	4 fach	Mixtur	4 fach
Scharff	4 fach	Kornett	2–5 fach
Kornett	3–5 fach	Oboe	8
Trompete	8		
Bordun	32		
Bordun	16		
Hohlflöte	8		
Gemshorn	8		
Gamba	8		
Doppelflöte	8		
Quinte	5⅓		
Fagott	16		

Oberwerk		*Echowerk*	
Prinzipal	8	Geigenprinzipal	8
Quintatön	16	Lieblich Gedackt	16
Rohrflöte	8	Flauto dolce	8
Viola di Gamba	8	Salizional	8
Flauto amabile	8	Unda maris	8
Gedackt	8	Lieblich Gedackt	8
Oktave	4	Oktave	4
Gemshorn	4	Zartflöte	4
Rohrflöte	4	Salizional	4
Quinte	2⅔	Nasard	2⅔
Waldflöte	2	Oktave	2
Terz	1⅗	Cymbel	3 fach
Sifflöte	1	Progressio harmonica	2–4 fach
Mixtur	4 fach	Äoline	16
Schalmey	8		
Stahlspiel	8		

Pedal	
Prinzipal	16
Salicet	16
Subbass	16
Oktave	8
Bassflöte	8
Oktave	4
Dulcian	16
Violoncello	8
Flöte	4
Grossnasard	10⅔
Terz	6⅖
Rohrquinte	5⅓
Kornett	4 fach
Mixtur	4 fach
Trompete	8
Klarine	4
Untersatz	32
Violon	16
Posaune	32
Posaune	16

(1843–1914), was an enthusiastic disciple of Liszt, and gave the first performance of *Ad nos, ad salutarem undam* there in 1855. Liszt wrote his *BACH* Fantasia for this organ in the same year. The main interest of the instrument, built in 1853–5 by F. Ladegast, is the presence of such a traditional element as a *Rückpositiv* with a large *Echowerk* (Swell) and the use of a Barker-lever action. The impressive richness of the tuttis and the wide variety of delicate colours would make this the ideal instrument for the Lisztian style of organ writing.

A curious instrument Liszt had made for his own use is the 'Orgel-Piano'. It has two manuals, the upper, a full 7-octave piano keyboard, and the lower, a divided harmonium keyboard. The manifold possibilities of this amalgam of sustained and percussive sonorities may well have influenced Liszt in his organ writing. The harmonium was certainly taken seriously by some late nineteenth-century French composers, notably Franck and Vierne, and the flexible and expressive possibilities of the instrument were undoubtedly of interest to Liszt.

The problem of versions and editions is important. Liszt left many passages that a virtuoso organist would want to play on the pedals laid out for manuals. The Margittay edition gives these original versions, but it is quite permissible for a player to choose other, more demanding, realizations, such as those by Dupré or Jean Guillou (b.1930). Best of all, the organist can use the originals as the basis for his own realizations. Such a procedure would be fully in the spirit of the romantic period, when players were still expected to be creative in their performances and the separation of composer and performer was still some way off.

Reubke

The true successor to Liszt was undoubtedly Julius Reubke (1834–1858), son of an organ-builder and a pupil of Liszt. His *Sonata on the 94th Psalm* is heavily indebted to Liszt's

Ad nos, but is arguably finer in its formal coherence and economy of structure. With this work the organ enters the realm of the symphonic poem, and the colouristic shadings of the romantic organ receive their fullest expression. The freedom of rubato and the sense of rhetoric we find in some movements by Mendelssohn and Schumann find their ultimate expression in these works of Liszt and Reubke. In their harmonically conceived fugal writing the problems of clarity associated with pre-classical organ music hardly arise.

It is noticeable that the German romantic organ composers, following the lead, or rather the absence of lead, of their baroque forebears, gave little or no indication of definite registrations. Organ-building was becoming so varied and experimental that composers clearly felt that much must be left to the individual performer. As much was said by Mendelssohn in the preface to his Sonatas.

The settled traditions of the German *Werkprinzip* and the French classical school were long past; the dynamic flexibility of the new piano and orchestra was the model. We shall see the impasse this situation was eventually to lead to in the work of Max Reger (1873–1916).

Brahms

With his interest in old music, especially that of Bach, Johannes Brahams (1833–1897) could hardly ignore the organ; his neo-classical leanings took him in the direction of the baroque forms of the prelude and fugue and the chorale prelude. His preludes and fugues recall the contrapuntal studies of Schumann, but the Eleven Choral Preludes, Op. 122, his last composition (1896), show a fascinating blend of Bachian style and a deeply felt personal idiom. The feeling of a pianist writing for the organ persists, even when the idiom is not far removed from baroque pastiche.

The use of the swell is certainly appropriate in the more

personal and expressive pieces, such as *Es ist ein Ros'
entsprungen*, and the final prelude, *O Welt, ich muss dich
lassen*. This last piece introduces a double-echo technique,
which was later to be used to the point of mannerism by
Sigfrid Karg-Elert (1877–1933).

Brahms's aching nostalgia for a golden past is mirrored
in the uneasy feeling evoked when we hear these preludes.
Is Brahms perhaps singing of a golden past of the organ
itself? These beautiful pieces may be introduced to the
student as a romantic counterpart to Bach's *Orgelbüchlein*.

Reger, Karg-Elert and Hindemith

With the work of Max Reger the cult of the monumental in
organ writing, adumbrated by Liszt, reaches its apogee. Of
course he was the contemporary of Strauss, Gustav Mahler
(1860–1911) and the emergent Second Viennese School
(who in general esteemed him highly). The predicament of
the organ and its music in the German tradition at the close
of the nineteenth century is encapsulated in the work of
Reger.

At a first glance it looks as though Reger is trying to
combine the virtuosity of Liszt with the neo-classical outlook of Brahms. His titles are usually baroque: Prelude or
Toccata and Fugue; Passacaglia, Chorale-Fantasia or Prelude – all these forms were cultivated by Buxtehude.
Unlike those by Liszt and Reubke, Reger's fugues really
are fugues – page after page of closely worked counterpoint, crammed full of scholastic devices, in which writhing
climax is piled on writhing climax. Even that is not enough:
the internal tension of the part-writing that served for the
pre-romantics must now be further heated and dramatized
by the use of dynamics and changes of tempo.

According to Reger, modern fugue must start slowly and
very softly (compare Liszt's *BACH* Fantasia); it must
increase gradually in speed and loudness and must end
triple or quadruple *fortissimo*. After all, his music seems to
say, Bach simply did not have the resources to realize the

emotional and dramatic potential of the fugue! Similarly, Bach hardly touched the fringe of chromatic possibilities in his fantasias for clavier and organ. After Liszt and Wagner these wild progressions can be taken to their ultimate frenzied conclusion.

The immense tonal resources of the late nineteenth-century German organ were to hand, but the requisite flexibility of tone was not. How could one avoid the addition and subtraction of stops by hand or combination pedal, or the necessity of using separate pedals for each enclosed manual division? The answer lay in the invention of the *Rollschweller*. This device adds and subtracts stops from the quietest to the loudest dynamic level: it is not too much to say that only with its use can the intentions of Reger be fully realized.

If the expressionist movement might be regarded as the final 'boiling over' of romanticism, then Reger certainly provides the most complete example of this in organ music. But whereas the concentration on subtlety of expression and an extreme dynamic range is quite legitimate in the orchestral music of Schoenberg and his school, the same approach, when applied to the organ, is self-defeating and leads inexorably to the electronic organ of the mid-twentieth century.

Reger had two distinguished disciples, Karg-Elert and Paul Hindemith (1895–1963). Karl-Elert continued further the search for flexibility of dynamic expression and freedom of chromaticism within a tonal basis, whereas Hindemith's three sonatas demonstrate a retreat from the excesses of romanticism to a twentieth-century neo-classical approach. We have to consider whether the work of Reger and Karl-Elert does violence to the essential nature of the organ. If we conclude that it does, then perhaps we have to agree that the future of the organ does lie in its past.

The best of Reger's music – and also the easiest to approach technically – is in his smaller-scale pieces. The *Benedictus*, Op. 59 No. 3, is a beautifully restrained example of his expressive style, suggesting a parallel with the slow movements of Anton Bruckner (1824–1896) and Mahler, while the Introduction and Passacaglia in D minor is the most convincing demonstration of his ability to integrate the romantic-rhetorical with the baroque. Both pieces are manageable on instruments of moderate size. Likewise, many of the chorale-improvisations of Karg-Elert may follow on logically from the preludes of Brahms.

The tonal ideal of the late nineteenth-century builders and composers was definitely the orchestra of Wagner and Strauss. A dark, blended sonority required many 8' stops of Principal, Flute and string quality, backed up by a reed chorus. Clarity of line and part-writing was no longer sought after, and the unyielding chorus of the classical organ was regarded as an outmoded relic of the past. If the instrument had been improved, then it followed that old music, including Bach's, must be interpreted in the current style – in other words, like Reger's. The romantic orchestration of Bach's organ music lasted for a long time, and there are many players today who will remember the style from their youth.

German and French traditions of organ music throughout this period maintained their characteristic features. The Germans cultivated large-scale contrapuntal structures, with an increased emphasis on rhetoric and drama; the French looked for clarity and brilliance of sound, an emphasis on colour as a structural element, and an objective, architectural approach that is based on the tonal design of the instrument itself.

Twelve
The Romantic Revival: France

No school of organ-building and organ composition has been more closely integrated than the French. The standardization of registration in the seventeenth and eighteenth centuries was to be paralleled in the nineteenth under the inspiration of one man, Aristide Cavaillé-Coll. His first important instrument was commissioned for the Abbey of St Denis, near Paris. Although a first scheme was submitted in 1833, the instrument was not finished until 1841, by which time Cavillé-Coll had radically altered his original conception.

The stop list of 1833 shows that he was still basing his work on the French classical tradition. In 1841 he introduced the newly invented Barker lever, which made a less straightforward layout of chests possible. Wind pressures were increased, and a wider scaling than the classical French was adopted. He introduced double-length harmonic ranks, especially reeds, and the chorus included Strings, Flutes, Principals or Montres and the Reeds. An important innovation was the placing of families of stops on to separate chests, each with its own wind pressure. These were controlled by ventils, operated by pedals, so enabling the organist to prepare registrations that could be rapidly added or subtracted as required.

Composers such as Franck, Widor and Vierne built their works around this new system of registration as readily as Couperin and Clérambault planned their pieces around the tonal structure of the classical instrument. In fact, many features of the Cavaillé-Coll instruments may be seen as continuing the classical tradition, to a much greater extent than the German or English romantic organs.

The *Grand Orgue* dominated, as it did in the classical scheme: there was never any question of more or less equally balanced choruses. The term 'terraced dynamics', which was thought in the early years of this century to be the right approach to the registration of baroque organ music, seems to be far more correct when applied to the nineteenth-century French school. Usually only three manuals were required: *Grand, Positif* and *Récit*, placed in ascending order, but giving a descending dynamic spectrum.

On the *Grand Orgue* the reed chorus dominated, with the brilliant support of the mixtures (including Cornets and Tierces), with the foundation stops providing warmth and support. It will be readily seen that this is, to all intents and purposes, a combination of the classical *plein jeux* and *grand jeux*.

The *Positif* was based on a secondary level of foundation stops, of a rather string-biased sonority, chorus reeds 8' and 4', and a solo reed, either a Cromorne or a Basson-Hautboy. The *Récit* was reed-based, like the *Grand Orgue*, but much lighter in tone and capable of a relative *pianissimo* with the box closed. The foundation stops on the *Récit* were string-based, but there would be Flutes 8', 4' and 2⅔', an Octavin 2', Basson-Hautboy and Vox Humana. A chorus reed 16' was often omitted, as in Franck's organ at Ste-Clotilde. The build-up through the three manuals would be:

    Récit   Fonds et Anches 8' and 4' (box closed) *pp*
    Positif   Fonds 8' and 4' + *Récit* *mp*
    Grand Orgue   Fonds 8' and 4' + *Positif* + *Récit* *mf*
    Récit box opened and *Positif* reeds added *f*
    Grand Orgue reeds and mixtures added *ff*
    Pédale reeds added *fff*

The reeds of a fourth *Bombarde* division, when present, could be added for a final chordal peroration. The manuals were normally coupled, as were the *Grand Orgue* and

Positif for the *plein jeux* and *grand jeux* in the classical tradition.

It will readily be seen, from this description, that the new orchestral organ of Cavaillé-Coll was still based on the earlier tonal structures. Another important residual feature was the emphasis given to solo stops of real strength and character, rather than imitative delicacy and blend. The Trompette, Cromorne, Vox Humana and Flûte stops of the eighteenth-century school were still there, recognizable, even if modified somewhat in the direction of greater fullness and warmth.

The new orchestral character of the French organ was soon to be exploited by the most important names of the rising school of composers – Franck, Widor and Vierne – in their aptly named 'symphonies'. The Germans still retained the term 'sonata' for their large-scale works, an indication that orchestral colour was of secondary importance to them. 'If you only knew how I love this instrument,' said Franck to the curé of Ste-Clotilde. 'It is so supple beneath my fingers and so obedient to all my thoughts!'

When playing music of the romantic French school it is vital to remember that organ and music were as inextricably linked as any in the whole history of the genre. Points especially to be borne in mind are:

The tonal characteristics of the Cavaillé-Coll organ;

The layout of the manuals;

The ventil system of changing groups of stops;

The use of dynamic markings in relation to the context of a given registration.

For instance, it is common practice for the *Récit* to be used with foundation stops and reeds throughout a whole movement, with dynamic markings of *pp* to *ff*. These refer only to the use of the swell shutters and not to the changing of stops. Furthermore, composers utilized to the full the possibilities of *sforzando* which the swell-pedal mechanism allowed.

The modern balanced mechanisms slow up the almost instantaneous opening and closing possible with the nine-

101

STE-CLOTILDE, PARIS

Grand Orgue		Positif	
Montre	16	Bourdon	16
Bourdon	16	Montre	8
Montre	8	Flûte harmonique	8
Flûte harmonique	8	Bourdon	8
Bourdon	8	Gambe	8
Gambe	8	Salicional	8
Prestant	4	Prestant	4
Octave	4	Flûte octaviante	4
Quinte	2⅔	Quinte	2⅔
Doublette	2	Doublette	2
Plein Jeu		Trompette	8
Bombarde	16	Clairon	4
Trompette	8	Clarinette	8
Clairon	4		
Récit		Pédale	
Viole de gambe	8	Quintation	32
Flûte harmonique	8	Contre basse	16
Bourdon	8	Flûte	8
Voix célestes	8	Octave	4
Flûte octaviante	4	Bombarde	16
Octavin	2	Basson	16
Trompette	8	Trompette	8
Basson-Hautboy	8	Clairon	4
Voix humaine	8		
Clairon	4		

teenth-century actions. This is yet another instance where technological 'improvements' militate against correct performance of the music. Instances of this technique are to be found in Franck's Final in B flat, and the *Final* from Vierne's *Symphonie III*.

Franck

Grande pièce symphonique, Op. 17
When considering the French symphonic tradition, Franck's *Grande pièce symphonique*, Op. 17, is a crucial

work to look at. This work virtually inaugurated the genre of the organ symphony, and it displays the strengths and weaknesses of Franck in full measure. The material is not always distinguished and the approach to structure often improvisatory, page 8 (Durand) being an example of the composer at his most helpless in matters of formal cohesion. He resorts to mere tinkering with registration of the most naïve nature in order to link his exposition and development sections, and this after a most powerful and convincing treatment of the first subject.

The four bars linking the *Introduction* to the *Allegro* demonstrate the addition of the reeds on *Positif* and *Grand Orgue* to effect a crescendo from *pp* to *ff*. In the *Andante* we may be surprised to see that the *Positif* Cromorne and Flûte is to be accompanied by *Récit* Fonds and Anches, but we have to remember that the Cavaillé-Coll *Récit* reeds were voiced very lightly and so capable of a relative *pianissimo*, and that the *Positif* solo reeds were bold in character. The use here of Cromorne with Flûte and Bourdon 8' is immediately reminiscent of classical practice, and is a further reminder of the continuing tradition behind the romantic organ in France.

The whole of this work might be a sketch for the orchestral Symphony in D, so it is not surprising to find Franck inserting a scherzo-like *Allegro* as the middle section of his slow movement. Here the indicated registration is quite unclassical:

Récit   Flûte 8'; Bourdon 8'; Clairon 8'
Positif   Bourdons 8' and 16'; Flûte 8'
Récit and *Positif* coupled

The writing is very pianistic, and, with the two manuals coupled, would not have been possible without the aid of the Barker lever.

The shadow of Beethoven hangs over the whole piece; most obviously in the introduction to the *Final*, where Franck parades material from the previous movements before settling on a major version of the first movement's first subject. The frequent changes of registration are

Organ

expedited by means of long-held pedal notes, but even so the composer probably needed the help of an assistant. Despite what I have said about the Cavaillé-Coll organs being rooted in the classical tradition, the differences are immense, and this work highlights them as well as any.

Pièce héroïque

A work, much shorter and finer, which shows the influence of piano and orchestral writing even more explicitly is the *Pièce héroïque* of 1873. This was composed for the opening of the organ in the Trocadero in Paris, and shows just how quickly the organ became secularized.

The use of reiterated chords is reminiscent of the Schumann Canon in B minor; here it is used to throb above a left hand on Fonds 16' and 8' in which cellos and basses unmistakably sing. The middle section is announced by a rhythmical motive on the pedals, suggestive of timpani, and a translucent woodwind colouring is given to the chorale-like theme with the use of Flûte and Bourdon 8' in the right hand, against Trompette, Hautbois and Flûte 8' in the left. This combination of the two reeds and Flûte was a favourite of Franck's, and it occurs over and over again in his work.

The blend of these three stops on the Ste-Clotilde instrument was obviously of striking beauty to Franck and is to be found in the *Cantabile*, where a *Tristan*-like chromaticism elicits a religious love song of restrained ecstasy – demonstrating yet again how well the 8' reeds of the *Récit* must blend with the Fonds of *Positif* and *Grand Orgue*. On organs of a different tradition the effect is often distressingly harsh.

These two contrasted piece make the best introduction to the work of Franck. Although not easy, they are sufficiently concise to be relatively accessible for a student at this stage.

Widor

The concept of the symphonic organ, well prepared by builder and composer, was soon firmly established in the work of Widor and his organ at St Sulpice, built by Cavaillé-Coll in 1857–62.

Although the core of Widor's work is contained in his ten symphonies, they are very different works from their model. There is a classical objectivity and a monumental calm in this music, which is quite different from the heated emotionalism of Franck. Not only the spirit of Bach, but baroque procedures are revived in Widor's work. The opening *Prélude* and the closing *Fugue* of *Symphonie I* are neo-classical exercises; the *Toccata* from *Symphonie IV* evokes the rhetoric of the early eighteenth-century French overture, while the *Fugue* that follows is completely baroque in spirit, without a trace of the romanticism that was to play such a part in Reger's work.

Admittedly Widor saw all organ music in terms of the Cavaillé-Coll organ: 'After Cavaillé-Coll came the proper playing of the works of Bach,' he wrote in his preface to André Pirro's *L'Orgue de Bach* (Paris, 1896). A somewhat different view emerges from his remarks in the preface to his edition (with Albert Schweitzer) of the Bach organ works: 'On the modern organ the player will do well to introduce a few shadings, in order that the listener may not be wearied by the reeds and mixtures.' Indeed, this edition, although it presents the text clear of editorial markings, makes innumerable suggestions as to manual and registrational changes.

The monumental Bach was the Bach most prized by the romantics. Clearly this concept was as much the force behind Widor's symphonies as the Franckian legacy of orchestral treatment, or Liszt's pianistic influence. Just as several of Bach's works show his desire to provide musical and technical examples for teaching purposes, so Widor saw his works as containing all the demands necessary for the new style of composition and performance.

Organ

Although his *Symphonie I* introduces a toccata-like style of writing – a single line of staccato semiquavers in the manuals with a more sustained line in the pedal phrases – his overriding preoccupation is with polyphony. This trait he shares with Reger, but whereas the rapid harmonic changes, chromatic intensity, and ceaseless contrapuntal activity is ultimately self-defeating with the German composer, Widor always strives for clarity and a basic monumental calm, far more suited to music for a large organ in a vast architectural space.

Although he possessed an extensive knowledge of the modern orchestra – his book on instrumentation was often consulted by Ravel – he made it quite clear that the geniuses of the two media were completely separate. His music can be very exciting as organ sonority yet somewhat superficial and banal in content (the *Final* from *Symphonie VI* for example). Yet the *Adagio* from the same work is deeply felt, without a trace of sentimentality. No wonder that it was a favourite of Fauré's at the Madeleine. This movement is registered for strings and Celestes on three keyboards from the outset, and its warmth of sound and elevated spirit does indeed recall the expressive sensuousness of a body of strings, without ever falling into the snare of mere imitation.

The *Symphonie Romane*, Op. 73, shows Widor looking forward, in his use of the plainchant *Haec Dies*, both to the world of Charles Tournemire (1870–1939) and Olivier Messiaen (b. 1908), and also back to the masses and suites of the eighteenth century. The textures are much thinner, and the upper register of the manuals is exploited in the interests of clarity and brilliance. (An interesting comparison between the French and German schools may be made by noting the use made of the treble clef for the left-hand stave.)

Guilmant

A more conservative contemporary of Widor was Félix

Guilmant (1837–1911), who retained the title of 'sonata' for his large-scale works. He did valuable work as an editor of pre-nineteenth-century French organ music. His editions, with Pirro, of Titelouze, du Mage, Marchand and others are still useful, and often the only ones available. His researches into old music gave him an insight into the need for a re-assessment of the romantic organ, and so helped to forward the movement for reform both in France and the rest of Europe.

Vierne

Widor's successor as a symphonist was Vierne, who occupied the post at the Cathedral of Notre-Dame in Paris for most of his life. His language derives from a combination of the intense chromaticism of Franck with the architectural strength of Widor; whose movements he frequently used as models for his symphonic pieces. Vierne is more detailed and imaginative in his registrational directions than Widor, and this emphasis on colour as a source of inspiration in his music points again to the work of Tournemire and Messiaen. A noteworthy instance is the *Intermezzo* from his *Symphonie III*, registered thus:

Récit   Gambes; Flûtes 8′ and 4′; Nasard
Positif   Salicional; Unda maris
Grand Orgue   Bourdon 16′ (accouplé au Récit)
Pédale   Bourdons 8′ and 16′; Flûte 4′

In the last line the *Pedal* Flûte is used alone in three- and four-part chords – an intriguing textural effect.

To my mind, an even more notable achievement than his six symphonies is to be found in the *Twenty-four Pieces in Free Style*, for harmonium or organ. Written on two staves, with pedal indications, these delightful pieces continue the tradition of harmonium composition that Vierne would have learned from Franck.

Many of the pieces make slender technical demands; they are probably the best available material for the initiation of a student into the world of French romantic organ music. They give useful practice in phrasing, registration, the use of the swell pedal, all encountered in music of charm and originality.

An important point in the interpretation of this school is the question of tempi and breadth of style. Just because the writing is so often influenced by pianistic ideas, and general style seems to demand a virtuoso approach, there is a danger that the tempo chosen will be too fast. It should be remembered that much of this music was conceived for a large organ in a resonant building. This must be allowed to influence choice of tempo and style to some degree, even when the work is to be performed in a relatively dry acoustic.

The music is often rhetorical and needs to be projected and pointed with freedom and panache. The first movement of Vierne's *Symphonie II* is a good example of this. Most of the important cadence points need to be broadened, and the resonance allowed to 'settle' before going on to the next phrase.

The question of music and acoustic is one that becomes really relevant with the large instruments of the late nineteenth-century, and the freedom and flexibility of the approach to tempo goes right through the French school from Franck to Messiaen. Even when the acoustic is not excessively resonant, it is necessary to adopt a relatively broad and free style in comparison with that demanded by, say, the sonatas of Mendelssohn.

Tournemire

This freedom of style is an even more important element in the music of Tournemire, who was a contemporary of Vierne; like him a pupil of Franck, and the latter's successor at Ste-Clotilde. In his fifty-one sets of pieces for the liturgical year which he called *L'Orgue mystique*, Tournemire is, in effect, reviving the organ mass of the seventeenth and eighteenth centuries. Improvisation on plainchant has always been a vital part of the French liturgical tradition; and in these pieces the composer provides music that is improvisatory in style, and the use of a harmonic language in which the influence of Claude Debussy (1862–1918) may be clearly discerned.

Dupré

Marcel Dupré succeeded Widor at St Sulpice. He links the world of Widor and that of Messiaen, and his music represents the culmination of the symphonic school. As is the case with his predecessors, his work is frequently dismissed as having little appeal or merit in the eyes of non-organists. It is music for players and *aficionados*, rather than for the general music lover. But this is probably true of many composers for, say, the guitar and the brass band too.

Dupré was among the most gifted improvisers of his generation. As a teacher and editor he followed in the steps of Widor and Guilmant, producing useful editions of early music, as well as revisions of the romantics, such as Liszt and Franck. Several of his works were written with students in mind, notably *Le Tombeau de Titelouze* and *Vêpres du Commun de la Vierge*, all based on liturgical themes. They are a modern equivalent of Bach's *Orgelbüchlein*, and are useful as technical, liturgical and concert material.

These works were almost certainly improvised during services before being written down, but the most astonishing feat of this kind took place in 1921, when Dupré improvised what was to become the *Symphonie-Passion* on the new organ in Wanamaker's store in New York.

Of course Dupré was not a 'classical' player, in the same mould as our eighteenth-century specialists of today. But it is easy to underestimate his contribution to the art of the organ as player, composer, improviser, editor and teacher.

Messiaen

Certainly the most important composer of the French organ school, Messiaen, makes no secret of his indebtedness to his teacher: many of the technical features of his early works owe a great deal to Dupré's music. The *Diptyque* is an obvious example. Despite this, Messiaen's music at once impresses by its originality. Yet it can still be related to the classical French tradition, and to the emotional idealism (and mysticism) of Franck.

Like Franck and Bach, Messiaen is a composer whose music stems both from a liturgical working environment and from an involvement in music for the secular environment of the concert hall. At the age of 17 he composed *Le Banquet céleste* and in it the authentic voice of the composer is to be clearly heard. In this the notes are not difficult to play, but the extreme slowness of pulse provides a valuable interpretation exercise for the student – how to get an overall sense of line and phrase at ♪ = 52 as well as offering a fresh insight into the essential nature of the instrument.

The organ is the only instrument on which tone can be so unyieldingly sustained that it gives an impression of time and eternity – an idea to which the composer was to give even more forceful expression in his *Apparition de l'Eglise éternelle* (1934). This is marked merely *Très lent* compared with the *Extrêmement lent* of *Le Banquet*, and no metronome mark is given. The composer issued a revised edition (in doubled note values) of *Le Banquet* when he became aware that it was being played too fast by organists who had forgotten the classical tradition of slow movements being notated in the shorter note values. In *Apparition* Messiaen leaves out time signatures and gives no indication of the pulse, though the harmonic idiom makes it clear that we must count in quavers.

Having been caught out over the correct speed for *Le Banquet* organists welcomed as a godsend the composer's own recordings of his organ works, issued in the late 1950s.

These made it clear that the composer rejoiced in extreme contrasts of tempo – his *vif* was indeed fast. In the case of *Apparition*, *Très lent* means a mark right at the top of the metronome, in the region of ♪ = 40–4. This may appear unbearably slow, until we realize that the composer is working out some of the possibilities of Wagner's late style, especially that of *Parsifal*: 'Thou seest, my son; here time becomes space,' Gurnemanz teaches Parsifal, as they enter Grail Castle. The three pages of *Apparition* have an eleven-minute duration, according to my timing.

These two short(!) pieces having given the student an insight into the mind of Messiaen, the larger work that immediately suggests itself for study is *L'Ascension*. Apart from a freshly composed third movement, this is a transcription of an orchestral work, but this is by no means immediately apparent. The outside movements are easily approachable via *Le Banquet* and *Apparition*, but the other two are best approached via the composer's piano preludes of the same period.

It is worth noting that the difficulties of Messiaen's organ writing lie mainly in the manual parts. The pedal parts are usually much simpler. Messiaen often uses the pedal for melodic purposes, but rarely for virtuoso effect. This, combined with the detailed nature of his registrations, in which colour is more clearly a vital element in his musical thought than of any composer since the baroque, places him firmly in the most venerable tradition of French organ music.

His imaginative and highly original use of colours often poses severe problems for players whose instruments are lacking in the stops required. Just as Franck found inspiration in his personal use of the Cavaillé-Coll organ at Ste-Clotilde, so Messiaen delights in his exploration of the sonorities of the much larger instrument at La Trinité. One example must suffice: the registration for *Joie et clarté des corps glorieux* – No. 6 from *Les Corps glorieux*:

Récit   Voix humaine (sans tremolo); Cymbale; Quintaton 16'; Clairon 4'

Organ

Positif Trompette 8'; Cornet et Montre 16'
Grand Orgue Diapason 8'
Pédale Flûtes 16' et 32'; tir. R.

This is followed by:

Positif Cromorne; Bourdon 16'; Tierce
Récit Hautbois; Quintaton 16'; Tierce et Piccolo
Grand Orgue unchanged

Then:

Grand Orgue Cornet
Récit Viole 8'
Pédale tir. R. seule

Only on the largest and most comprehensive instruments might one expect to find such a wide range of colours available *on the right manuals.*

Compared with the problems posed by the French school of all periods, it is true to say that Bach's music is relatively effective on almost any kind of organ, large, small, with an action mechanical, pneumatic or electric. Nevertheless, Messiaen's music is so important that an acceptable approximation of his requirements is worth seeking, and it is usually possible to find one.

Messiaen's interest in organ colour has increased with his output, and *La Nativité* of 1935 is less exploratory in this respect than *Les Corps glorieux* of four years later. Movements from both of these cycles are possible for the student who has assimilated the ideas behind *Le Banquet* and *Apparition*, and has done some work on the composer's piano writing, for example in the song-cycles *Poèmes pour Mi* (1936) and *Chants de terre et de ciel* (1938). As is the case with Bach and Franck it is true that one can hardly hope to play Messiaen's music well without a deep and persistent study of his works for other media.

Messe de la Pentecôte (1950) and *Livre d'orgue* (1951) are better left to a later stage in the student's development, but the most recent cycle *Méditations sur le mystère de la Sainte Trinité* (1969) contains movements, such as the sixth and eighth, which present such a startling synthesis of his earlier and later styles that they must be recommended to the serious student of Messiaen at a fairly early stage.

Perhaps the final point to be made about Messiaen's contribution to the organ is that the most original organ composer of the twentieth century has based his art on the nineteenth-century organ of Cavaillé-Coll, not on a revival of the classical organ. As much as Liszt and Franck he relies on a flexibility of tone that owes its inspiration to the piano and orchestra, but still has its roots in the organ of the French classical tradition. As yet the classical organ has not produced a similar inspiration for fresh and exciting composition.

In comparison with Messiaen's towering achievement the work of the rest of the French school is apt to seem relatively unimportant. Toccatas of varying degrees of refinement and sophistication have been written by Henri Mulet (1878–1967) and Maurice Duruflé (b.1902), and the brief career of Jehan Alain (1911–1940) produced some work of distinction and of even greater promise. His two chorals, *Dorien* and *Phrygian*, make the best introduction to his style and easily follow the study of some of the Vierne *Twenty-four Pieces*.

Demessieux

The technical side of French organ writing, especially notable in the work of Widor and Dupré, receives its fullest expression in the *Six Etudes* (1946) of Jeanne Demessieux (1921–1968). Although manual prowess is firmly tested, the great value of these pieces lies in the emphasis given to the development of pedal technique. In this way they provide material hardly to be matched elsewhere.

The First, for alternate toes, develops evenness and control of touch, as well as a feel for the spacing of different intervals. The Second (for thirds) again concentrates on the pedal part, the objective here being a perfect legato and precision of attack. The Third (for sixths) develops the same qualities as the Second, but also concentrates on flexibility and relaxation of the leg muscles. The Fourth is concerned with alternating chords – a frequent device in modern organ writing; again, perfect control of evenness of attack and legato is the aim. The Fifth (repeated notes) is one of the most valuable of pedal studies, ensuring looseness of the ankle, the precision of attack. All the techniques dealt with are summed up in the Sixth Etude (for octaves).

Simultaneousness of attack, relaxation of the ankles, as well as complete control of staccato release are thoroughly tested in these exacting pieces. They are, as Dupré points out in his preface, conceived for the modern organ with electric action, permitting lightness and ease of touch, even with all three manuals coupled. The techniques they develop are not directly related to the classical school of organ performance, except possibly the first (for alternate toes), but they certainly sum up the technical developments which took place in France during the last hundred years. Allowing for the limitation of being based on a technical exercise, they are far from being musically arid, and they can be used to good effect in concert.

Guillou

The concert approach to the organ has been most strikingly upheld by Jean Guillou, who followed Marchal at St Eustache in Paris. His Toccata of 1966 exploits the percussive possibilities of the organ in a way reminiscent of early Stravinsky and Bartók. The same reliance on dissonant ostinati is much in evidence in two works based on literary sources: *Le Chapelle des abîmes d'après Julien Graq* of 1972, and *Scènes d'enfant d'après The Turn of the Screw* of 1975. The spirit of Lisztian romanticism looms large in these works, and we are not surprised to find Guillou producing a 'realization' of the *Prelude and Fugue on BACH*, intended as an evocation of the way the composer might have elaborated his score in performance.

Thirteen
The Romantic Revival: England and America

England

S. Wesley

Early nineteenth-century music in England was dominated by two overwhelming Continental influences: Handel and Mendelssohn. But there was a lone voice, Samuel Wesley (1766–1837), who based his art on an admiration for the music of J. S. Bach. His devotion was independent of the Bach revival initiated by Mendelssohn in Germany; indeed, by then, most of Wesley's work was complete. But his study of Bach meant that the voluntary idiom, with its somewhat lightweight, Italianate charm, could be enriched and deepened with a more searching use of counterpoint and chromaticism, as well as with elements of the *galant* style of Bach's sons.

It must be remembered, though, that the full implications of the Bach style could not be realized in English organ music because of the lack of a Pedal division and balanced choruses. Indeed, a comparison of organ specifications of the second half of the eighteenth century and the early years of the nineteenth, such as that undertaken by Francis Routh in *Early English Organ Music*, shows that English organs were moving further away from the classical ideals of clarity and translucence of tone. The trend became one towards an accompanimental instrument, and one more capable of simulating orchestral sonorities.

By comparison with the trends on the Continent, much of Wesley's work is apt to appear old-fashioned. But when

Organ

SURREY CHAPEL, BLACKFRIARS ROAD

Great		Swell	
Open Diapason I	8	Down to tenor F	
Open Diapason II	8	Open Diapason	8
Stopped Diapason	8	Stopped Diapason	8
Principal	4	Principal	4
Flute	4	Cornet	III
Twelfth	2⅔	Trumpet	8
Cornet (Treble)	III		
Sesquialtera (Bass)	II	Pulldown pedals, 1½ octaves	
Mixture	II		
Trumpet I	8		
Trumpet II (*Sw*)	8		

assessed on his own terms, he is seen to represent a significant development of the English voluntary style. Until quite recently, little of his work was in print, but the opus 6 Voluntaries, edited by Francis Routh, are now available. These pieces were probably written for the organ in the Surrey Chapel, Blackfriars Road, built by Elliot (date uncertain).

The pedal pulldowns permitted some textural extension, but the main interest of these Voluntaries lies in the number of movements, sometimes three or four, and the more extended structures adopted, occasionally suggesting the sonata style of the Viennese school. Some passages are notated in block chordal form, especially the codas; these need to be elaborated with some improvisation techniques. Wesley was one of the outstanding improvisers of his generation and his works offer useful scope for the player willing to take this art seriously today.

S. S. Wesley
Wesley's son, Samuel Sebastian (1810–1876), was one of the first organists to absorb the rising importance of Continental romanticism in England, led by the music of Mendelssohn. Furthermore, he carried the development

of the organ as an independent accompanimental instrument a long way.

His *Choral Song and Fugue* is an original conception, the chordal and lyrical first movement being paired with an exuberant fugue based on a subject from James Nares's anthem 'Ascribe unto the Lord'. The freely ranging modulations and the keyboard idiom used take this work a long way from the style of Nares's own voluntaries. The climactic build-up in this movement is as exciting as any in Mendelssohn's organ music, and, given a more firmly grounded English organ tradition, shows what S. S. Wesley might have achieved in this field.

The movement that gave the greatest impetus to English organ-building in the nineteenth century was the new wealth and civic pride of the industrial towns of the North and the Midlands. The new town halls required organs to accompany the flourishing choral societies of this period, as well as to bring the orchestral repertoire to the attention of people who rarely had an opportunity to hear an orchestra.

With very little awareness of the Continental traditions of organ-playing and composition, English players were highly pleased with the new role of town musician. As their style of playing was based on orchestral imitation, it is not surprising that they should attempt to apply the same techniques to Bach and Handel as they did to Mendelssohn and Wagner. Given the musical conditions in England at the time, this approach was inevitable, and builders were quick to identify the need and to answer it.

Technological developments proceeded and builders addressed themselves to the problems of providing:

Actions that were light and responsive in dealing with the figurations of orchestral transcriptions, with manuals coupled;

A range of imitative stops, such as Clarinet, Oboe, Cor Anglais and Flute, which were as lifelike as they could get;

117

Swell boxes that would give the dynamic range expected of a player on the above instruments, and that could produce the *pianissimo* of muted strings, together with a crescendo on a reed-dominated swell chorus that could rival the Wagnerian horns and trombones; the balanced swell pedal was invented;

Higher wind pressures for the reeds, both solo and chorus, so that evenness of tone throughout the range from bass to treble was possible, thus ensuring that the tutti of the organ would now be reed-dominated, just as the tutti of the contemporary orchestra was brass-dominated.

Orchestral instruments at this period were being improved along the lines of easier control, smoothness and increased roundness and volume of sound, and organ registers were 'improved' with the same objectives in mind. Just as wind-players concentrated on the production of tone that 'began from nothing', so the attack sound or 'chiff' was eliminated.

The organ that Henry Willis built for the 1851 Crystal Palace Exhibition set the pattern for the rest of the century in England. It had three manuals and a Pedal division with seventy stops. The Swell Organ had twenty-two stops, a clear indication that it was the second manual in importance, with the Choir Organ pushed into an uncertain role of a few soft accompanimental and solo stops.

Previously W. Hill had built Pedal divisions under the guidance of H. J. Gauntlett which must have been modelled on some Continental examples – Haarlem has been suggested. The organ of Great George Street Chapel, Liverpool, built in 1841, had a forward-looking specification with the normal Continental compass. But where did the idea of Tierce mixtures on the Pedal come from? To help out the limited Pedal reeds? Many organs of this period had a few notes only of reeds, with often but an octave compass for the flues. There was, too, much controversy over the merits of the old GG compass as opposed to the Continental-influenced CC. Both Hill and Willis were

GREAT GEORGE STREET CHAPEL, LIVERPOOL

Open Diapason	16
Bourdon	16
Principal	8
Fifteenth	4
Sesquialtera (3⅕)	V
Trombone	16
C–d′	

influenced by Cavaillé-Coll, and Willis's instrument for St George's Hall, Liverpool (1855 and 1867) set an entirely new standard for English organ-building. For the first time since the Middle Ages, English organs had caught up with Continental thinking.

The St George's Hall organ could play the classical repertoire as effectively as the contemporary St Sulpice instrument; it was superb for the new French school, and it was unsurpassed as a medium for orchestral transcriptions and for accompaniments. But where was the new English music to be played on it? In fact there was none of any significance. There was no tradition of important organ composition as in Germany and France, where only a Mendelssohn or a Franck was awaited to lead a renaissance.

ST GEORGE'S HALL, LIVERPOOL

Great	16.8.8.8.8.8.8.5⅓.4.4.4.4.3⅕.2⅔.2.2.II.V.IV.16.8.8.8.4.4.
Choir	16.8.8.8.8.8.8.4.4.4.2⅔.2.2.IV.8.8.8.4.
Swell	16.8.8.8.8.8.8.4.4.4.2.2.2.2.II.V.16.16.8.8.8.8.8.8.4.4. Trem
Solo	16.8.8.4.2.16.8.8.8.8.4.8.8.8.4.
Pedal	32.32.16.16.16.16.8.8.5⅓.4.V.IV.32.16.16.8.4.
Compass:	GG–a″, Pedal C–f‴

119

Organ

Elgar

For its first organ masterwork, comparable in quality with the French symphonic productions or the large works of Reger, England had to wait until 1895 when Edward Elgar (1857–1934) composed his Sonata in G, Op. 28. Orchestrally conceived, it is effective only on the new-style instruments of Hill, Willis and G. D. Harrison.

Just playing the notes is technically demanding, but the problems of organ management are even more intractable. It was composed for the organist of Worcester Cathedral, Hugh Blair, to play for a visiting delegation of American organists. Blair confessed to having 'made a terrible mess' of it, but this is excusable as he had insufficient time adequately to prepare a work which made such unprecedented demands on instrument and player.

The *Intermezzo* and *Larghetto* can be adapted to a two-manual instrument, and may be tackled by a second-year student who is prepared to study the Elgarian style as revealed in the *'Enigma' Variations*, written three years later, and the two symphonies. Some commentators, disliking the orchestral organ *per se*, have questioned the value of this Sonata. Whatever one thinks of the influences that gave birth to it, its beauty and importance cannot be denied.

WORCESTER

Great	16.8.8.8.8.8.4.4.2.16.8
Swell	16.8.8.8.8.8.4.4.2.16.8.8.8.8.4.
Choir	16.8.8.8.8.8.4.2.8.8
Solo	8.4.16.8.8.8.
Pedal	64.32.32.16.16.16.16.8.8.32.16.16.8.

25 couplers
Compass: C–f′–c‴
Electric action

The virtuoso organist could now find instruments to compete in variety and range of tone with the virtuoso orchestra of Wagner and Strauss. When Willis commented of the double-Venetian-front swell at Gloucester Cathedral (1847) that its *pianissimo* was simply astounding', he meant that the organist could at least match or even surpass the delicacy of tone required of a first-rate orchestra; a worthy aim indeed, given the aesthetic climate of the times. Presumably he would have wished to find its full organ similarly astonishing.

The year after Blair gave the first performance of the Elgar Sonata at Worcester, the Cathedral organ was rebuilt by Robert Hope-Jones (1896). Hope-Jones's invention of the Diaphone enabled the same basic pipe to be used either as a flute or a reed. A thick, opaque sound characterized the Hope-Jones instruments, which utilized the new ideas of the 'unit chest' and the 'extension organ', whereby a relatively few ranks of pipes could provide a stop list of twenty or thirty times their number.

The console could be placed at any distance from the pipes. Sound of any dynamic level, with apparent variety of pitch and timbre, was now cheaply available. This new technology was to lead the way, first to the cinema organ and eventually to electronic instruments. The Elgar Sonata can be regarded as a brilliant 'one-off' essay, as an expression of the musical possibilities of the orchestral organs of Hill and Willis before the traditional basis of such instruments was threatened by the new technology.

Parry and Stanford

The main Continental influence on English music at this period was German, especially that of Mendelssohn and Brahms. The neo-classical tendencies of both composers were followed by Parry and Charles Villiers Stanford (1852–1924).

Parry's chorale preludes are Bach seen through the richness of a Brahmsian textural haze. With these thick textures and the typical instrument of the period, it is not surprising that the composer cried in desperation, 'The organ is the very devil to write for!' This outburst was provoked by the experience of hearing Walford Davies try out passages from his newly composed Preludes at the Temple Church in 1913.

Parry was doubtless bemused by the inadequacy of the English organ of the period to articulate the abundance of contrapuntal detail that the Continental pre-romantic instruments would have coped with easily. Compared with those of his contemporary Reger, his textures are models of clarity and restraint. Although there is a complete absence of the violent expressionism found in much of Reger's work, his pieces are the nearest equivalent to the aims and achievements of the Teutonic master. The best introduction to Parry is to be found in the Elegy and the more delicate chorale preludes, such as *Melcombe*.

Stanford based some of his Preludes and Postludes on Gibbons's hymn tunes: the 'voluntary' concept of service music was now being fertilized by the more liturgically based tradition of Protestant Germany.

Vaughan Williams
The most gifted student of Parry and Stanford was Ralph Vaughan Williams (1872–1958); his contribution to the repertoire comprised *Three Preludes on Welsh Hymn-Tunes* and a Prelude and Fugue in C minor. There is a neo-classical approach in the last; it is modelled on Bach's work in the same key and form, BWV 546, and is said to have been inspired by Harold Darke's playing of Bach at St Michael's, Cornhill.

A study of the registrations suggested is an apt reminder of the way in which the Bach piece might have been registered by an English organist of the 1930s. The fact that it was later scored for orchestra is presumably an indication that the composer found the organ just as devilish to write for as Parry did! The *Welsh Preludes* are an extension of Bach's (and Parry's) techniques and can serve as beautiful studies for a second-year student.

Howells

A more esoteric development of the liturgical link is to be found in the Psalm-Preludes of Herbert Howells (1892–1983). Each is a reflection on a verse from the Psalms and they represent the most refined treatment of the orchestral resources of the English cathedral organ. Howells's idealistic and sophisticated approach to the instrument might be described as impressionistic. It is certainly reliant on atmosphere and the subtle use of the organ in a (preferably) resonant acoustic.

His music, dependent as it is on a lavish supply of registrational aids to ensure flexibility of tone and dynamics, is the absolute antithesis of the classical organ idiom. Despite this it is genuine organ music, and would be virtually impossible to transcribe for any other medium. The Psalm-Preludes are variable in interest; the student should begin with two examples – the second of the First Set, and the third of the Second Set.

If you admire this music then you have to admire the organs – Gloucester Cathedral, for instance – that evoked it. To separate the value judgement of the music and of the contemporary organ is pointless: the aesthetics are inseparable. Most English organ composition since Howells has used the organ in a similar way, with some influence from the French school, especially from Messiaen; but Howells sums up the romantic revival in England.

America

In America the Episcopal Church was the mainstay of organ music in New England during the first quarter of the nineteenth century and English tastes and styles were the natural basis for what was played and composed. Later the influx of immigrants meant that Germanic influences prevailed, to be eventually overtaken by the French school, as the work of Franck and his disciples became known.

Ives and Schoenberg

Charles Ives (1874–1954) reacted against German acade-
micism and his *Variations on 'America'* provide a much
needed antidote to the accepted ideas about 'good taste' in
organ music. His integrity and originality won enthusiastic
appreciation from Arnold Schoenberg (1874–1951) (himself an immigrant academic) who made his sole contribution to the repertoire with his *Variations on a Recitative*,
Op. 40 (1941).

It is regrettable that this work is generally known only in
a heavily edited version (for the organ at Princeton University) by Carl Weinrich. The style derives from Reger in its
textural and expressionistic leanings and the tonality is a
heavily chromaticized D minor. Schoenberg expects the
same flexibility of tone and dynamics as did Reger, and a
classical approach will not suit this music at all, in spite of
its characteristic neo-classicism of form and expressionistic
content. Until a new edition enables us to get closer to
Schoenberg's intentions, the *Variations* will remain a very
problematic work. The best approach will certainly be via
Reger's late works.

Hindemith and Heiller

The neo-classical side of Reger also lies behind
Hindemith's three sonatas, which appeared between 1937
and 1940. Hindemith's sympathy with the baroque aesthetic is apparent in these sonatas, which are modelled on such
baroque structures as ritornello, aria, fugue and fantasia.
The textures are always light and transparent, but the
phrasing often conflicts with dynamic changes, and it seems
that the composer still expected the flexibility of sound of a
modern instrument, with at least one enclosed division.

The registration of these works presents many problems
of this kind: whereas Sonata No. 1 seems to have been
written with a large orchestral organ in mind, the other two
suggest more of a chamber organ approach as most
appropriate. The second movement of Sonata No. 2 is a
good introduction to the Hindemith style and shows a

composer thinking of his music in terms of an old sonority: the use of *Hauptwerk* and *Oberwerk* is indicated. This kind of writing is analogous to a modern composer writing for harpsichord, recorder or viol consort and represents something quite new in organ music.

The Sonata of Anton Heiller (1923–1979) derives from the Hindemith examples but is clearly laid out for the instrument by a virtuoso exponent of the classical style.

Organ-building in America has always been so dependent on European ideas that there is little to be said on the topic, other than to point out that the first real growth of interest coincided with the development of the romantic organ in Europe. The affluence of the new country meant that all the imported ideas could be carried to their logical (or illogical) end. For instance, Hope-Jones's innovations found their ultimate fruition in the Wurlitzer. Similarly, when the change of taste took place, the availability of finance meant that America could lead the way in the classical revival, which culminated eventually in the present interest in historical copying.

Fourteen
The Twentieth Century: The Classical Revival

At the same time as the application of ever-advancing technology was taking the organ further away from its original design principle of mechanical action from key to pipe, the beginnings of musicological research in Europe, under the leadership of German scholars, ensured that considerations of 'authentic' performance practice and the historical study of instruments would eventually result in a return to those first principles in organ design.

The increasing interest in J. S. Bach's music meant that the harpsichord and clavichord, the clarino trumpet and the oboe da caccia and the oboe d'amore would be studied, restored and copied, and the organ could not expect to escape this trend. Many old organs were still standing; some had been altered or 'improved' to some degree, but others were virtually unchanged since the end of the eighteenth century.

Moreover, although Bach sounded mightily impressive on the Cavaillé-Coll in St Sulpice, or on the Willis in St George's Hall, Liverpool, it was becoming ever clearer that Bach's work should be considered in the context of earlier composers – Buxtehude, Scheidt, de Grigny, Frescobaldi and the rest – and their works sounded distinctly odd on instruments that were designed to thrill audiences with Elgar's *Imperial March* or the *Toccata* from Widor's *Symphonie V*.

The scholars insisted that this music was good and worthy of modern ears, so maybe there *was* something wrong with the town hall and cathedral organs. Comments such as Paul Henry Lang's 'Its colossal range and great variety of colour combinations made the organ the baroque instrument par excellence,' and 'The nineteenth-century organist, long estranged from true organ music...' and 'Since the baroque era the organ has lacked a true repertory,' were bound to give pause to musicians if not to organ-builders. Lang was writing in *Music in Western Civilisation* at the same time (1940) as Hindemith and Schoenberg were composing their organ pieces but, forty years earlier, Guilmant's editions of classical French masters and Schweitzer's books on Bach were also pointing to a re-assessment of both the music and the instrument.

At first, tonal design seemed of more importance than the action used – the idea of 'progress' in mechanical matters died hard – and it was a long time before the crucial importance of a *good* mechanical action was realized in practice. The siting of the instrument also came in for consideration. So many nineteenth-century instruments in England and America were crammed into small chancels or side chapels from where only a tightly muffled sound could emerge. The casing of the organ as an integral element of its resonating structure and its positioning in the building were more fully understood.

Those monastic foundations reconstituted as cathedrals in England after the Reformation presented an especially difficult problem from this point of view. Where a cathedral retained its screen, dividing the choir from the nave, the organ remained *in situ*, usually a small two- or three-manual instrument with the Chair Organ projecting into the choir. While such organs retained the modest dimensions of the seventeenth and eighteenth centuries, all was well. Such organs were accompanimental instruments, designed to be heard from the choir and not intended to 'fill the building'.

In places where the screen was taken down the organ was placed at triforium level in the choir itself, usually over-flowing outside any nominal casing as it was successively rebuilt and enlarged. (The two things usually went together.) It is impossible to contain and project the sound of such a spread-out scheme as is now common, but the apparent logical solution of two organs – one placed against the west wall for organ music and congregational singing, and another in the choir for liturgical services – remains literally a pipe dream. In any case, the accompaniments of the nineteenth and twentieth centuries require the resources of the large organ, and no cathedral is likely to be able to afford two instruments adequate for their respective roles and to some extent duplicating each other.

Here theory and practice part company and until organ theorists engage with practical problems little useful advice will be forthcoming. As the theorists are usually in universities and the practitioners are in cathedrals there is a great gulf between them which appears unlikely to diminish. The choral services will continue to be held in the choirs of the cathedrals and the organs will be sited so as to be in the closest proximity to the musicians they are meant to accompany.

From a disregard of such considerations has emerged the 'museum' organ (discussed in chapter sixteen): an excellent tool for the study of the music and performance practice of a historical period, but of little use outside the museum. An English cathedral organist needs, nay, *wants* to be able to play Thomas *and* Simon Preston; Tallis *as well as* Howells's *Master Thomas's Testament*; not to mention Purcell, Stanley and Parry, together with Bach, de Grigny, Franck and Messiaen. From such a predicament has arisen the idea of the 'eclectic organ', a concept that deserves a chapter to itself.

The classical revival, then, has resulted in the study of organs in relationship to the music associated with them, and has also concerned itself with the careful preservation and restoration of old organs, bearing in mind that many such were rebuilt and enlarged as frequently as nineteenth- and twentieth-century instruments. It has meant the building of organs with classical stop lists, but detached, electric-action consoles, such organs often exchanging Hope-Jones

8′ fog horns for screaming, scalping mixtures, equally unbearable in Bach or Boëllmann; it has produced the eclectic organ on which 'it is possible to play absolutely anything'; finally it has given rise to the historical copy for the museum. It has also resulted in huge four-manual organs in which the tracker action is so heavy that the much vaunted potential for intimate contact between finger and pipe is remote, if not non-existent.

Of course all this had to happen, but the solutions to the problems posed by organ history are far from obvious or simple. Should one play the French Suites of Bach on the piano? Probably not. Should one play the Liszt Sonata on the harpsichord? A foolish idea. Should one play Bach on the Albert Hall organ? Should one play the Franck *Pastorale* at the St Laurenskerk at Alkmaar? (I have heard it there.) Or Frescobaldi at Alkmaar? Or Couperin? It is time to consider the eclectic organ.

Fifteen
The Eclectic Organ

In 1850 William Hill installed an organ on the north side of the choir in Ely Cathedral. Typically for the period it has no Pedal division, and it was placed inside a new case by Sir Gilbert Scott who had removed the ancient choir screen on which previous organs had been placed. Scott's case was 'inspired' by that in Strasburg Cathedral, which, unusually for a Continental church, has the organ suspended from the north wall of the nave, two-thirds of the way down. It was enlarged by Hill in 1871 and a Pedal Division added.

In 1908 Harrison and Harrison built an entirely new organ, incorporating much of Hill's pipework, but mainly revoiced. The resulting instrument was a splendid embodiment of the 'cathedral orchestral organ' concept of the early twentieth century in England. Its smoothness and richness of tone was indeed Wagnerian or Straussian in its mellowness and homogeneity, and it was perfect for English organ music from Elgar to Howells.

The Trombas had the blending quality of Wagner tubas, but they were not really right for French romantic music: they certainly dominated, if not obliterated, the chorus

---

ELY CATHEDRAL

Four Manuals (61 notes)   Pedals (32 notes)   69 stops

Great		Swell	
Sub Bourdon	32	Lieblich	16
Gross Geigen	16	Echo Gamba	8
Contra Clarabella	16	Vox Angelica	8
Open Diapason I	8	Open Diapason	8
Open Diapason II	8	Lieblich	8
Open Diapason III	8	Lieblich Flöte	4
Hohl Flöte	8	Principal	4
Geigen	8	Fifteenth	2
Wald Flöte	4	Sesquialtera	V
Geigen Principal	4	Horn	8
Octave	4	Horn Quint	5⅓
Quint	5⅓	Oboe	8
Octave Quint	2⅔	Vox Humana	8
Super Octave	2	Double Trumpet	16
Mixture	V	Trumpet	8
Harmonics	V	Clarion	4
Trombone	16		
Tromba	8		
Octave tromba	4		

Choir		Pedal	
Double Salicional	16	Double Open Wood	32
Open Diapason	8	Double Stopped Diapason	32
Salicional	8	Open Wood	16
Gedackt	8	Open Diapason	16
Dulciana	8	Sub Bass	16
Flauto Traverso	4	Salicional	16
Salicet	4	Stopped Diapason	16
Dulcet	2	Violone	16
Dulciana Mixture	III	Flute	8
		Violoncello	8
Solo		Octave Wood	8
Contra Viola	16	Bombardon	32
Viole d'orchestre	8	Ophicleide	16
Viole Celeste	8	Posaune	8
Viole Octaviente	4		
Cornet de Violes	III		
Harmonic Flute	8		
Concert Flute	4		
Cor Anglais	8		
Orchestral Hautboy	8		
Clarinet	16		
Tuba	8		

work, but not with the snarling brilliance of Cavaillé-Coll, whose reeds almost spat at the hearer. The mixtures, although there were ten ranks of them, could not supply the colourful shimmer of the French Fournitures and Cornets. French classical music was quite out of the question, but Bach was possible, though best played up an octave, basing the chorus on the 16′ Double Diapason. This procedure not only gave a cleaner and more convincing chorus, but also had the merit of keeping the left hand and pedal parts well separated, in the interests of clarity. An independent pedal was not possible, but this procedure was an effective expedient.

The urge to play a much wider repertoire more convincingly (if not 'authentically') was there. There was no hope of a rebuild in the foreseeable future so inevitably the desire to make a few changes oneself could not be resisted. Simply by changing pipe positions it was possible to provide a Cornet from the Choir mutations – a fresh meaning for this word! As easily done was the retuning of the Dulciana against the Gedackt, and the Salicional against the Open Diapason to make an Unda Maris and a Fiffaro respectively. How strange that it was the demure and unassuming Choir manual that seemed most ripe for this ravishment, all done at no cost except the tuner's time. The eighteenth century was now more of a possibility, and a Frescobaldi *Toccata per l'Elevatione* sounded remarkably good. (Of these changes the Unda Maris and the Fiffaro were retained in the 1975 major rebuild.)

When in the early 1960s some emergency action was necessary to keep the instrument usable, a few further changes were slipped in. Harrisons' removed the ultra-smooth Tromba tone from the Great and Pedal reeds, which were now more fiery and exciting, but also much louder so that the balance between them and the mixture chorus was rather less satisfactory than before. But a Cliquot-type *grand jeux* movement, as well as a Vierne *symphonie*, now became a really stirring experience.

This was the Ely sound people missed when a thorough-going rebuild was undertaken in 1975. The new reeds were carefully balanced so that the 16' and 8' could be used with the Principal chorus in Buxtehude and Bach *plenum* registrations, and the 8' and 4' with the Cornet to make a *grand jeux*. Alas, the Cremona on the Choir (balanced in power with the Positive Cornet) had to cover both German Krummhorn and the French Cromorne requirements.

Ought I to have left the 1908 organ as it was, well suited to Harwood and Bairstow, Elgar and Howells? Perhaps I should have opted for a copy of a Renatus Harris double organ – with a small Pedal division to balance? Why add a Pedal division – for the German baroque school? In any case, the Harris chorus is not the same as the Schnitger or Silbermann sound. And how would such an organ accompany Howells's *Collegium Regale* or support a congregation of a thousand or two?

The answer is, of course, that a large church or cathedral needs a large eclectic organ, so sited that it can be accommodated easily (visually) within the building, and so suitable for both choir and nave services. Such an instrument is there primarily to be *useful* and the usefulness of a cathedral organ is determined by very different criteria from that appropriate in previous eras and liturgical traditions.

This argument will seem obvious and unanswerable to many people, but because it is so easy to criticize the eclectic concept without any genuine consideration of the practical factors in its favour it is necessary to restate it at this point. A move away from eclectism in the direction of an acceptance of 'some stylistic limit' (Peter Williams) in an instrument – a situation true even with the most eclectic of instruments anyway – leads inescapably to 'some kind of historic copy' and so to the 'museum' organ.

It remains to be seen what composer is likely to be inspired by a historic copy. The great organ composers, such as Bach, Franck and Messiaen, have been inspired by the fine instruments of the tradition they have grown up in, but something of a dilemma is posed by the organ trends of today. How is the past to be understood for the future?

Sixteen

The Museum Organ?

Musicologists soon recognized the peculiar suitability of the organ as a subject for their investigations – not just because the organ is among the oldest instruments known to civilized man, nor because its repertoire is the largest of any instrument and so much of it falls significantly into the 'early music' category, but mainly because no other instrument has been made in such a variety of forms and sizes. And, although many old organs still survive, they have rarely survived in an unaltered condition. All this offers an intriguing challenge to the scientific enquirer after musical truth. The idea of restoring an instrument to its 'original' condition is essentially a modern one, resulting from the rapid and ever-increasing growth of 'historical consciousness'.

The story of St Bavo's Church in Haarlem is a good example of the kind of fate that used to befall organs. There is a splendid painting of 1636 which depicts a magnificent Gothic instrument of exceptional grace and beauty. This organ was removed in the early eighteenth century, when the wealthy burghers decided that their town church deserved a more up-to-date instrument of a size and importance comparable with any in northern Europe. Ostensibly this is the organ that can be seen today. It was played by Handel and Mozart, but, as it has been renovated and 'improved' several times, it cannot be regarded as an authentic early eighteenth-century instrument.

Rare instances do exist of an instrument being left musically unchanged but cosmetically brought up to date with new casework. But of course this operation may have altered the tonal projection of the organ. An example of this kind of up-dating is to be found in the Church of S. Petronio in Bologna. As I write, the St Bavo organ is undergoing yet another 'restoration': this time aimed at as accurate a reconstruction of the early eighteenth-century instrument as careful research can ensure.

The Organ Reform Movement

The organ reform movement began with attempts to build instruments with tonal schemes 'suitable for Bach'. As the importance of the work of his predecessors and near contemporaries became more appreciated, so the idea of the 'baroque' organ took hold of organists' and builders' imaginations. Further investigations revealed that, tonally speaking, the 'baroque' organ included many radically different types, depending on geographical location. There were many variations of tonal concept in Germany alone, but much greater contrast was found between organs in Italy, Spain, France, England and the Netherlands. Compositional influences may have travelled widely and readily but obviously the instruments themselves could not.

Today we want to savour the 'right' sounds in a Frescobaldi toccata, a Cabezón tiento, a Buxtehude prelude and fugue, a Couperin *offertoire* and a Purcell voluntary – yet the single organ that could provide these very different tonal spectrums would be a monstrous impossibility rather than a wondrous machine. Hence the eclectic, or universal, organ, capable of playing all schools in a general sense, but none with any real character or personality. French reeds of either seventeenth- or nineteenth-century provenance fail to blend with German eighteenth-century mixtures. The Vox Humana is too loud for Franck but not sufficiently telling for Couperin or John Stanley. The foundation stops usable in Bach are quite wrong for Vierne; and so on.

The answer, of course, is to build historical copies which

are concerned not just with tonal schemes and mechanical actions but also with the correct historical ideas of temperament, winding, compass, size of key and pedal board – in short, concerned about everything that could possibly have a bearing on the relationship of the instrument to the music. Such an instrument is necessarily restrictive rather than general in its usefulness, and this is why churches and concert halls, needing to encompass a wide repertoire as part of their daily life, do not commission such instruments. So we find that the only place where historical copies of organs can be easily funded and appreciated is in the natural home of scientific enquiry and cultural appreciation: the university.

As in the case of the St Bavo instrument, where old instruments are concerned the watchword today is restoration rather than rebuild. A point has been reached where the organ is viewed as a historical phenomenon, just like the harpsichord or the fortepiano or the pianoforte, with nineteenth-century technological developments either eschewed completely, or else applied on a strictly limited basis. It is nevertheless true that a historical copy is just that, and its self-imposed limitations restrict it to the university 'museum' as an instrument for study rather than wide-ranging performance purposes. There is no way around this impasse. To suggest that builders revert to a kind of primeval or even medieval unsophisticated innocence of tone in which there shall be neither Spanish, Italian nor German influence, evades the issue of genuine character as much as the 'universal' instrument does.

Tuning and Temperament

As with the provision of a steady wind supply and a non-mechanical action, the nineteenth century readily accepted the idea that equality of temperament was yet another instance of a natural and inevitable progression towards eradicating the 'faults' of old instruments. But, as with the other cases cited, musicological investigation has come to suppose otherwise, and only a complete and thorough-going enquiry into the problem will serve as the basis for opinion and decisions in any given case.

The history of all Western keyboard tunings from 1450 is concerned with the attempt to retain the purity of the third with the utilization of all twenty-four triads possible in the twelve-note octave. Before the mid-fifteenth century the Pythagorean system of tuning by pure fifths had suited the needs of medieval music admirably, and the resulting wide major thirds were not considered detrimental for a musical language still based on the modal system and the perfect consonance. As the interval of the third began to play an increasingly important role in the gradual evolution towards the diatonic tonal system, musicians became more interested in the purity of the major thirds, thereby necessitating the tempering (narrowing) of the fifths.

The variety of tunings that resulted from the experimentation during the Renaissance period was eventually designated 'mean-tone' and one of these tunings became widely adopted: the 'standard' ¼-comma mean-tone, a temperament having eight pure major thirds. This is the tuning for the Brombaugh organ at Oberlin described below, though it is expanded by the use of the split keys beyond the normal limits of mean-tone, thereby giving three additional pure major thirds: on B, F sharp and A flat.

It will be understood that the main aural characteristic of this system is the multiplicity of pure major thirds, together with the resultant distinction between small and large semitones, both elements combining to create a character very different from the many well-tempered systems of the eighteenth century and the equal temperament of the nineteenth in particular.

The rise in popularity of the 'standard' mean-tone temperament coincided with the development of the practice of figured bass and a language based on a vertical harmonic system. It may be seen how the harmonic language of the early seventeenth century was based on the exploitation of the tensions created by such dissonances as the diminished fourth, F sharp – B flat, and the striking melodic character given to chromatic writing by means of the wider and narrower semitones. The harmonic language of the period cannot be fully understood and enjoyed through the unthinking acceptance of equal temperament as the only medium for its expression.

The lack of enharmonicity in the mean-tone system was overcome in the Oberlin organ by means of split keys. The late seventeenth century saw many attempts to devise a tuning that would permit the more remote tonal relationships sought by composers of this time, and in 1691 Werckmeister introduced a new theory of tuning which he called 'wohltemperiet', utilizing both wide and narrow fifths. Werckmeister's temperament offered the full range of keys and complete enharmonicity, and had the added advantage over the much later equal temperament of the presence of the all-important range of key colours his system retained from the earlier mean-tone tunings.

Instead of a uniform sameness of sound, whatever the modulation effected, each key level achieved offered a different colour character. For instance, the already striking Neapolitan sixth towards the end of Bach's Passacaglia and Fugue in C minor does not simply sound like a chord of C major transposed up a semitone but offers a dramatic colour in addition. In fact, our concept of key, in both colour contrast and modulatory use, acquires an entirely new significance, as does our understanding of pre-nineteenth-century music.

It is natural to ask why the various well-tempered systems were dropped in favour of equal temperament. It would appear that, with the ever-increasing use of chromaticism throughout the nineteenth century, such clearly defined key colours began to obtrude as not only irrelevant, but a positive nuisance. Just as smoothness and blend of sonority became a preoccupation of such composers as Wagner and Strauss, so the all-pervading chromaticism demanded a comparable smoothness and equality of tuning, thus allowing the greatest ease in rapid modulation.

As tonality began to lose its identity so did clarity of key colour and distinct character. Unequal tuning, then, can be justified in pre-nineteenth-century music, and in early nineteenth-century music which is firmly rooted in classical tonality – such as some works by Mendelssohn, Schumann and Brahms. One assumes that Brahms, with his classical leanings and love of the natural horn, would have found much to interest him in the revival of interest in early tunings. It must be agreed, though, that equal temperament is just as 'historically correct' for Liszt, Franck, Reger and Schoenberg, and indeed for any modern music that does not use key as an essential functional agent.

Historical Copying

It is only natural that most of the concentration on the copying of historic models should find a place in the 'new world' countries of North America and Australia – countries which draw on Europe for a large part of their cultural heritage and are not sufficiently ancient to have old instruments of significance from their past. Economic conditions have also played an important role as well. The university institutions in these countries have not as yet experienced the withdrawal of funds from interesting enterprises that has become such a prevalent hazard of intellectual life in Western Europe.

European organists have reason then to be grateful to those 'new world' musicologists whose labours may well lead to a more profound understanding of the history and nature of their 'old' instruments than is obtainable even from the much 'restored' originals.

The instruments discussed here vary considerably in the rigour of the 'historical copying' approach adopted. In other words there is often some element of compromise still present, to a greater or lesser degree.

Organ

Duke University, USA
A good example is the 1976 Flentrop organ at Duke University, Durham, North Carolina, which mixes eighteenth-century Dutch-style reeds with copies of Clicquot's 1782 reeds at Souvigny. This organ is sited in the orthodox west-end position and it seems that a nineteenth-century French organ is planned for the chancel end of the chapel. Clearly finance is no problem at Duke for there is a 122-rank Aeolian Skinner still standing in the chancel chamber. Presumably this has already achieved the status of a historical curiosity, but whether it will in future years be preserved, restored or merely copied is still largely a matter for conjecture. At any rate the Cavaillé-Coll instruments have now reached antique status and the Duke copy will no doubt include the Barker-lever-assisted mechanical action.

Monash University, Australia
A more recent but still compromised 'museum' organ is the 1980 instrument built by Jürgen Ahrend for Monash University, Australia. This scheme has the by now almost standard combination of a basic North German conception, with the addition of a number of colours from the French baroque organ 'that were found to be compatible'. The 'museum' character of the organ is confirmed by its non-suitability for music after Bach, with the possible exception of Mendelssohn. The pedal board is flat and short; the keyboard compass authentic (C – f'''), and the temperament unequal (Werckmeister II revised by Ahrend). There is no swell division but there are shutters to the *Brustwerk*. The tremulant affects the entire organ; flexible winding and suspended mechanical action is used.

McGill University, Canada
For a virtually non-compromise conception, the 1981 organ at McGill University, Montreal, Canada is worth consideration. This was designed by the Canadian builder Hellmuth Wolff and is patterned almost entirely on eighteenth-

140

MONASH UNIVERSITY, AUSTRALIA

Hauptwerk		*Oberwerk*	
Praestant	8	Praestant	4
Cornet (c')	V	Gedackt	8
Bordun	16	Quintade	8
Hohlflöte	8	Rohrflöte	4
Oktave	4	Nasat	3
Spitzflöte	4	Waldflöte	2
Quinte	3	Terz	1⅗
Oktave	2	Nasat	1⅓
Gemshorn	2	Scharf	IV–V
Mixtur	IV–VI	Trompete	8
Zimbel		Cromorne	8
Dulzian	16		
Trompete	8	*Brustwerk*	
Vox humana	8	Holzgedackt	8
		Holzflöte	4
Pedalwerk		Oktave	2
Praestant	16	Terz	1⅗
Subbass	16	Quinte	1⅓
Octave	8	Oktave	1
Gedackt	8	Mixtur	III
Oktave	4	Rankett	16
Flöte	2	Regal	8
Mixtur	IV		
Posaune	16	*Kornettwerk*	
Trompete	8		
Trompete	4	Cornet V (c')	
Tremulant to entire organ		Manuals: 54 notes (C–f''')	
2 Zimbelstern		Pedal: 30 notes (C–f')	
Shutters to *Brustwerk*		Couplers: *Ob/Hw*; *Hw/Ped*;	
Wind pressure 79mm		*Ow/Ped*	

Temperament: Werckmeister II revised by Ahrend

century French models. It is thought to be the first of its kind to be built on the North American continent. But, although the character of the manual divisions is historically correct, the Pedal division is of the kind that would have been found only in the larger and later of French eighteenth-century instruments and can therefore

141

McGILL UNIVERSITY, CANADA

Grande-Orgue
(2nd manual, C–g‴)

Bourdon	16
Montre	8
Bourdon	8
Prestant	4
Grosse Tierce	3⅕
Nazard	2⅔
Doublette	2
Tierce	1⅗
Fourniture	IV–III
Cymbale	III
Cornet	V
Trompette	8
Clairon	4
Voix humaine	8

Pédale
(C–f′, anches AA–f′)

Bourdon	16
Flûte	8
Gros Nazard	5⅓
Flûte	4
Grosse Tierce	3⅕
Flûte	2
Bombarde	16
Trompette	8
Clairon	4

Positif
(1st manual, c–g‴)

Dessus de flûte	8
Bourdon	8
Prestant	4
Nazard	2⅔
Quarte de Nazard	2
Tierce	1⅗
Larigot	1⅓
Fourniture	III
Cymbale	II
Cromorne	8

Récit
(3rd manual, f–d‴)

Bourdon	8
Prestant	4
Cornet	III
Hautbois	8

Couplers: *Pos/GO*; *GO/Ped*; *Pos/Ped*;
Tremblant fort
Tremblant doux
Rossignol
Wind Pressure: 75mm
Temperament after d'Alembert

be used in the German repertoire. The Pedal reeds go down to AA and two boards are provided: a French classical, and a straight flat one for German music. The key action is suspended and based on ideas of Dom Bédos, as are most of the pipe scales. The wind pressure (75mm.) can be increased by one-third when greater stability is required.

St Mark's on the Campus, Nebraska
The Italian Renaissance organ has usually been neglected

ST MARK'S ON THE CAMPUS, LINCOLN, NEBRASKA

Great		*Positive*	
(60 notes, C–c⁗)		(60 notes, C–c⁗)	
Principale	16 I–II	Flauto	8
Ottava	8	Flauto	4
Ottava	4	Flauto*	2
Fifteenth*	2	Cornetto†	III
Ripieno†	V	Rossignol	Tremulant

Pedal		Couplers: *GO/Ped*; *Pos/Ped*;
(29 notes)		*Pos/GO*
Contrabass	16 (from G)	
Ottava	8 (from G)	* First position of double draw
		† Second position of double draw

in favour of the German-French tradition, but a step in the direction of Italy has been taken at St Mark's on the Campus, Lincoln, Nebraska. This instrument, by Gene Bedient, is far from being an authentic historical copy, but it does concentrate on the tonal scheme of a typical Italian fifteenth–sixteenth-century instrument on one of its two keyboards. Instead of the nine flue ranks on the Great manual having separate stops, they are contained in four, and there is no Piffaro or Voce Umana, an undulating Principal rank, tuned sharp. But attention has been given to the pipe materials (high lead content) and the wide scalings characteristic of early Italian organs. The low wind pressure of 40mm., made possible because of the absence of reeds, creates a gentle fullness and sweetness of sound quite different from other national schools of organ design.

This then is still a partially eclectic instrument, which combines Northern European casework, and an eighteenth-century French-inspired action with an Italian Renaissance tonal scheme. Whereas the old organs would have had short-compass Pedal pulldowns, Bedient has provided a full-compass board, with 16' and 8' ranks taken from the Great. The temperament is Kirnberger III.

Organ

University of Vermont, Burlington
Charles Fisk is an important North American builder who
has shown an increasing interest in the construction of
instruments that incorporate features of old design other
than the use of tracker action and tonal schemes. His organ
for the University of Vermont at Burlington is French
inspired rather than a non-compromise copy, but its overall conception is rewarding to study.

Although the organ stands on the floor of the auditor-
ium, it was thought desirable to separate the *Positif* from
the Great and this was done with the aid of cantilevers. The
Great façade was suggested by the Robert Clicquot organ
at St Louis des Invalides in Paris. Suspended mechanical
action with a stop action including several double-drawing
knobs is used. Pipe scales are from Dom Bédos with reeds
based on the Clicquot organ at Poitiers. The 16′ Pedal
Bassoon is an exception, Germanic in style and intended
mainly for use in seventeenth- and eighteenth-century
German music.

Possibly the most interesting feature of this instrument is
the winding system. Fisk has followed Silbermann's practice, which was itself based on French eighteenth-century
practice. Instead of the nineteenth- and twentieth-century
custom of having one or more bellows for each division of
the organ, the eighteenth-century practice was to use one
large cuneiform bellows which feeds into a 'wind tree'
which then branches out into a large number of wind
chests. So, instead of a uniformly stable wind pressure,
whatever demands are made upon it, there is a fluctuating,
constant variation which removes one more mechanical
'constant' from the organ, replacing it with a system that
seems to 'live' and respond to the music. A uniform hard-
ness of tone is replaced by a live 'breathing' warmth, as
vital to the performance of pre-nineteenth-century music
as is tracker action.

All the essential ranks are present on the manuals for the
performance of French baroque literature, notably the
'Grand Jeu de Tierce' based on the Double-stopped

Diapason 16'. The Pedal lacks the Clarion 4' that would be present in a classical organ of this size but does include some extra stops for the performance of German music; namely Prestant 16', Night Horn 2' and the 16' Bassoon. The top keyboard is used solely for the short-compass five-rank Cornet de Récit which begins at Middle C. The wind pressure is 65mm. and the unequal temperament is after Werckmeister II.

Oberlin College, Ohio

The 1981 organ built by John Brombaugh for Oberlin College, Oberlin, Ohio, has been spoken of by Harald Vogel as the 'most outstanding instrument yet built in the twentieth century'. It is not an exact copy of any one extant instrument but is inspired by the important developments in organ design that occurred during the first half of the seventeenth century in North Germany.

It is extremely modest in size, thirteen stops over two manuals and pedals; the casework is inspired by Renaissance models and is flanked by large wing-like doors which can be closed to modify the tone, giving it a more gentle Italianate quality. Care over winding techniques of the period extends as far as the reversion to human energy to pump the two large, single-fold bellows. If this is not available an electric blower can be substituted. As noted also in the Vermont instrument by Fisk, the mechanical wind system bestows a fragile bloom on the tone giving it a riveting quality quite different from the unwavering uniformity of most modern instruments.

A further aid to its distinctive sound is provided by the mean-tone tuning employed. This tuning system involves the use of three split black keys – D sharp/E flat, G sharp/A flat, and A sharp/B flat – thus allowing the use of almost all the harmonic relationships used in the seventeenth century.

The dimensions of the keyboards permit a much greater range of intervals to be encompassed by the average hand. This is yet another thoroughly practical reversion to

Organ

OBERLIN COLLEGE, OHIO

Great			Brustwerk		
Praestant	8		Regal	8	
Gedackt	8		Hohlquinta	3 (treble)	
Oak Principal	8				
Octava	4		Tremulant to whole organ		
Spitzpype	4		Wind pressure: 78mm		
Sesquialtera	11		Winding from two wedge		
Quinta*	3		bellows (foot pumping or		
Octava	2		electric blower)		
Mixtura	V–VII		Pitch 1'c = 557 Hz.		
Trommett	8				

Pedal		
Subbass	16	
Praestant	8 (GT)	
Trommett	8 (GT)	

Coupler: *GO/Ped*
Compass: *Great* CDE–c''' with sub semitones† (56 notes, 15
    notes per octave)
    Brustwerk C/E–c'''.008' (45 notes, 12 notes per octave)
    Pedal CDE–d' with subsemitones (28 notes, 15 notes
    per octave)

* The double-drawing stop-knob brings on the Sesquialtera, which speaks from
middle C or C sharp (determined by a lever position), at the half-way position.
The fully drawn position allows the Quinta alone to speak throughout the
compass.
† The split keys are arranged so that E flat, G sharp and B flat play from the
front section of the key, while D sharp, A flat and A sharp play from the rear
section.

seventeenth-century practice which certainly aids the performance of this repertoire. This feature of the instrument,
together with the light, shallow action of the keys, makes it
ideal for the study of the relationship of early fingerings to
the music of the period. The concept of 'good' and 'bad'
notes – the strong and weak beats being intimately related
to what were considered to be good and bad fingers –
encouraged the student to relate the choice of fingering to
the music and especially the rhythmical construction of the

music. This completely changes our modern concept of keyboard fingering as a matter purely of comfort and convenience.

The organ is pitched in *Chorton* (baroque choir and organ pitch), a semitone higher than today's universal $A = 440$. Its extremely well-focused sound is very bright, transparent and lively and the possible variety of colourful combinations creates a range of effects that have been likened to the presence of a complete Renaissance wind band in the organ loft.

The functional necessity of the 'museum' organ is a question that is bound to arise. Is the instrument to be regarded mainly as a historical relic, or rather as a vital vehicle for new musical thinking? Before answering that question, it is necessary to decide what the essential nature of the organ is. Historical copies make available instruments of limited musical repertoire but of great usefulness in the study of the organ, both in its essential nature and in their assistance towards an understanding of any one particular manifestation of that nature. There will always be a tension for builders, composers and players between the concept of an 'organ for use' in the large concert hall and the cathedral and the limited historical copy for the serious scholar (which category might well include builders, composers and performers) in the museum. The conflict is evident in the instruments considered here, even with their already limited usefulness, but the stimulus they provide, an impetus towards fresh thinking about the instrument and its true nature, is a necessary counterbalance to the hitherto largely unchallenged concept of ever-increasing application of the latest technology to an essentially simple, though still wondrous, machine.

Seventeen
Modern Organ Music: The Present and the Future

The many types of organ discussed in preceding chapters make it obvious that the modern composer of organ music is confronted by a bewildering variety of styles and national traditions. The increasing interest in the pre-nineteenth-century instruments – for affinities with the harpsichord rather than with the piano – may lead him to agree with Schoenberg's verdict, expressed in his letter of 10 May 1949 to Dr David of Berlin: 'If one did not remember the splendid organ literature and the wonderful effect of this music in churches, one would have to say that the organ is an obsolete instrument today.'

Of all instruments the organ seems to be the hardest for a non-player composer to approach, and much of the most successful writing comes from players working in a clearly defined tradition, with a few stimulating works coming from leading composers from outside the organ loft.

Three main trends are discernible:

The neo-classical;

The development of recent styles of a traditional type, and

The use of aleatoric and other non-traditional pro-cedures.

The first two trends frequently merge: the synthesis of neo-classical and expressionistic, tonal and non-tonal elements in Reger's style is further developed in Schoenberg's *Variations on a Recitative*, and the Hindemith sonatas are not entirely purged of nineteenth-century influences. But a great deal of neo-classical writing still persists, much of it designed to be played on old instruments, or modern, classically inspired organs.

Anton Heiller draws on the music of Reger, Hindemith and Schoenberg for inspiration. He is a noted performer of the German school and a keen adherent of the *Orgel-bewegung*, and his works are the successors to the Hindemith sonatas and concertos in approach to the instrument; but they display a much stronger practicality in details of manual changes and registration. The second movement of the First Sonata is for manuals alone, and the third is a *Toccata* of the German classic type, rather than the French romantic.

A fellow Viennese and disciple is Peter Planyavsky (b.1947) whose works follow Heiller in attempting to provide music in a contemporary tonal language for organs of classical tonal design. Dynamic markings are scanty or absent; the swell is not utilized, and registrations are comprehensively indicated.

The expressionistic influence of Schoenberg is most fully realized in terms of the organ in the *Fünf Stücke* by Michael Radulescu. Here the writing has much the same rhythmical complexity to be found in the *Livre d'Orgue* of Messiaen, with as much emphasis on colour as a structural element – albeit colours to be found in the German classical instruments.

Piet Kee (b.1927), who plays regularly both the Schnitger organ in the St Laurens Church in Alkmaar and the Müller instrument in the St Bavo Church in Haarlem, has written much idiomatic music for the classical instrument, mostly based on old forms such as the chorale fantasia and the chaconne. It may be an editorial, rather than the composer's, marking, but one is surprised to find such a solecism as a crescendo indication on the last chord of a piece, when both hands and feet are fully employed. Howells, yes; but Piet Kee?

Whereas neo-classicism in music was a phenomenon of the twenties and thirties in the overall scene, it is a comparatively recent one in organ music, apart from in the music of those composers of the school who wrote only one or two works for the instrument. The Concerto of Francis Poulenc (1899–1963); the Hindemith sonatas; the *Neuf Préludes* of Darius Milhaud (1892–1974); the *Prelude and Fughetta* of Albert Roussel (1869–1937) and the *Fugue and Chorale* of Arthur Honegger (1892–1955) are examples of variable importance. Generally, the finest organ music has come from practitioners of the instrument – musicians who really understand its genius, strengths and limitations.

There is no doubt that the revival of the classical instrument and a truly contemporary repertory make very uneasy bedfellows. It is not unlike the situation with regard to the harpsichord: how many composers feel drawn to write for that instrument? Where is the modern repertoire for the viol consort? Modern music surely needs modern instruments, or at least instruments that seem sufficiently part of a living tradition.

Certainly I was inspired by the Alkmaar organ to write a prelude and fugue for it, and I have composed a trio sonata with the classical organ in mind. Nevertheless I do not see much future for the neo-classical style in composition, unless we use the word 'classical' in its spiritual meaning. Organ music can certainly well do without the ego-based romantic spirit, but even in the nineteenth century Widor was subjugating this to a more architectural and objective approach in his symphonies. Music as inspired decoration, rather than self-expression, or as an expression of a divine order – this must be the spiritual basis of the new organ music, and it is already present in the music of Messiaen.

Organ music as sonoral decoration – a range of textures, sonorities and dynamics – has been taken up by some composers, perhaps under the inspiration of the 1961–2 *Volumina* by György Ligeti (b.1923). Here, the tonal possibilities of the mechanical-action organ are exploited in an entirely non-classical manner, simply as a sound spectrum. *Volumina* has had few successors, but a combination of traditionally notated and aleatoric procedures has produced some interesting works.

Modern Organ Music: The Present and the Future

The *Chromatic Poem* of Sergey Slonimsky (b.1932) is a notable example of this type of writing, although dynamics, phrasing and registration are mainly left to the performer. Swedish composers have taken a lead in the imaginative use of the possibilities of the classical organ. In *Pour Madame Bovary* and *Eternes* by Jan Morthenson (b.1940) the performers play on the stop knobs, using varying positions, and so altering the wind pressures. The keyboards are used for sustaining pitches, generally by means of wedges or weights, and the piece begins from silence with the starting of the organ motor.

Equally radical are the ideas of Bergt Hambraeus (b.1928), who has combined electronic tape with organ. Some of the finest modern organs have been built in Sweden, where the state is responsible for the upkeep of the churches. Interestingly, this situation has coincided with a lessening of interest in traditional liturgical music, such as that based on chorales, in favour of concert music of a decidedly avant-garde nature.

It is here in fact that a new and convincing role for the classical organ has been tried: many of these 'texture' pieces are unplayable on the electric-action instruments. A dramatic illustration of this was provided by the scheduling of *Volumina* at the Royal Festival Hall in London: an attempt to start the work was frustrated by a fusing fault affecting the entire instrument. However effective or appropriate the electric switch type of action may be for Bach, it is clearly not well suited to Ligeti!

A notable fusion of classical and avant-garde elements is to be found in the work of the American composer William Albright (b.1944). His *Organbook 1* is a recreation of the eighteenth-century French *Livre d'orgue*, which, according to the composer, 'implies a collection of relatively short works, each of which deals with a sonoral aspect of the instrument and a particular type of composition'. Organ composition of this kind offers three challenges to the performer:

A new sound-world, radically different from the

harmonic and polyphonic textures, predictable rhythms and phrase structures to be found in the traditional languages;

New forms of notation, which may be the composer's own invention, or simply unfamiliar from lack of experience; and

New playing techniques, involving, for instance, hand positions different from those carefully cultivated for older music. Just as in early French music the indicated registration provides the character of the piece, so in Albright's work timbre is of far greater structural importance than any elements of melody and harmony.

In my *Symphonia Eliensis*, composed for the opening of the rebuilt Ely organ in 1976, the particular sonorities of the main choruses, as well as more individual effects, governed the character of each movement. In addition, each movement corresponds to an architectural aspect of the building; the movements are further related by the use of a plainchant melody, long associated with a hymn to St Etheldreda. The internal sections may be played in any order, just as one may look at a building from many viewpoints. Much use is made of note-clusters, and the player is allowed considerable rhythmic freedom.

This freedom of temporal realization is a further performance aspect that links old and new music. There is a strong affinity between, for example, the unmeasured preludes of Louis Couperin (*c.*1626–1661) and twentieth-century aleatoric techniques. Few English composers have written organ music of this nature, but *Games* (1977) by Paul Patterson (b.1947) is an interesting example. In this some use is made of conventional notation, but much of the layout is expressed graphically. Patterson's previous organ works are all conventionally notated and derive mainly from French romantic and more recent models.

Generally speaking, though, English organ music is still very traditional in outlook and is often intended for liturgical rather than concert use. The approach of Kenneth Leighton (b.1929) is not essentially dissimilar from that of Howells. The harmonies are more astringent; the rhythms more taut; the counterpoint more angular and wiry, but the sound-world is the same.

The influence of the French school is to be found in the work of John McCabe (b.1939), William Mathias (b.1934) and Bryan Kelly (b.1934). Their works are intended for the English eclectic organ, now to be found in many cathedrals and concert halls.

In Czechoslovakia Petr Eben (b.1929) speaks with an individual voice, in an idiom that can be related to that of Leoš Janáček (1854–1928) in its impassioned and often frenetic romanticism. Intensive motivic treatment of motives derived from melodic material of folkloristic origin is characteristic of his music; *Sunday Music* and *Laudes* are especially striking. *Laudes* makes use of plainsong material in each of its four movements. A large three-manual instrument with an enclosed division is needed; the writing within these resources is extremely idiomatic.

What of the future? As the tendency towards organ-building based on classical principles grows, so composers will be drawn to exploit those features of the organ that are peculiar to it: its range of colour and registers; its unique sustaining power; its old association with both religious and secular occasions and, above all, its essential spirituality, an unrivalled medium for the expression of timeless and universal ideas of man and his place in the scheme of things.

The organ is not at its best when it attempts to express the agonies and ecstasies of ego-dominated modern man. The crisis at the end of the nineteenth century, so vividly captured in the tormented expressionism of Reger, is a frenzy of writhing polyphony, tortured chromaticism, and the ultra extremes of dynamic contrast possible with the crescendo pedal. It can express the terrible in human life with an inexorable force unmatched elsewhere, but, as Mozart pointed out, it must still remain music, subject to laws of design which satisfy the mind, just as human life is governed by an inexorable law that operates in spite of, or precisely because of, human desires and emotions.

Organ music is at its best when dealing with spiritual themes. It is the God-instrument, not simply because it is used in churches but because of its intrinsic *nature*. The composer of the twentieth century who has most convincingly demonstrated this is undoubtedly Oliver Messiaen.

Although his work is rooted in the French romantic tradition, Messiaen's organ music is essentially classical in the sense that he takes man beyond his egocentric existence to realms of universal philosophy. It is this spiritual attitude that links him so firmly with Bach. The idea of imitating eighteenth-century textures, rhythms and formal designs never occurred to Messiaen – unlike his immediate predecessors, Les Six. Nevertheless, Messiaen's spirit is essentially classical, and the structural rigour of his music is but one aspect of this. More important is his non-egoistic approach to composition: it is this, rather than any technical features of his work, that makes him the most significant organ composer of his time.

Neo-classical organ music, concentrating, as it does, on using materials from the past in a superficial manner, may harmonize well with the classical organs, but the creativity which it demonstrates is inevitably of less importance than music that points forward in its development of contemporary thought. For example, the baroque fugue was a genre that grew from vocal roots, was transferred to the keyboard, and reached the culmination of its development in the hands of J. S. Bach. The harmonic-polyphonic language of which the fugue was the highest expression was ideally suited to the baroque organ, with its virtues of brilliant clarity and sustaining power. No other instrument or 'tool' can give such vitality of expression to the patterns of dissonance and resolution on which this language depends.

There is polyphony in Messiaen – see *Le Mystère de la Sainte Trinité*, No. 7 of *Les Corps glorieux* – but it is not couched in the empty shell of the baroque fugal style. No, the way forward for organ music is not through a neo-classical idiom. Similarly, the experimental sonoral composers who have radically re-assessed the possibilities of the mechanical-action organ have liberated our imaginations, and much may still be done in this field; but I think that the new resources will find their most appropriate use in 'controlled aleatoric' music, for sectional, colouristic effect, rather than as a main structural procedure. Chance may appear to play an important role in human affairs, and the 'sound' of music is indeed an indispensable element of it, but chance can never give complete and final expression to the truly classical concept of a divine order. Herein lies the highest function of the organ and the true divinity of music.

Eighteen
The Organ with Other Instruments

To some extent this topic overlaps with that of organ accompaniment, depending on the degree of independence in the role of the instrument; but its use in ensemble with voices and instruments must be as ancient as the instrument itself, both in a church and a domestic setting, and certainly predates its emergence as a solo instrument in Western Europe. The concertato style of the early baroque makes its use obligatory in liturgical music, and its use in church instrumental music continues at least as far as Mozart's church sonatas. These lightweight, but charming examples of *Kapelmusik* well demonstrate the gradual emancipation of the organ from its supporting role to one of complete independence.

J. S. Bach neglected the organ as an independent solo colour with other instruments. Its obbligato use is occasionally found, in *Cantata 27* for example, but the only concerto-like writing is in the well-known Sinfonia to *Cantata 29* of 1731. Apart from providing yet another demonstration of Bach's reliance on string techniques as the basis of his organ style, this is the sole example of Bach inviting comparison with the Handel concertos. Perhaps Bach felt that the organ, the 'Consort of them All', rendered the orchestra superfluous, because of the dominating character of the instruments he used. At any rate the combination of large organ and orchestra has remained an uneasy one to this day, and the creation of the organ concerto was left to Handel.

Handel

The size and character of the instruments appropriate for Handel's organ concertos is crucial for a correct performance. Regrettably it is a consideration frequently, and sometimes wilfully, ignored. The specification by Handel cited earlier was similar to that used by him for the performance of his concertos at Covent Garden Theatre. (Though Handel presented a two-manual, 21-stop instrument for use in the Foundling Hospital Chapel, he did not use it for concerto performances, so far as is known.) Handel wanted the intimate, chamber quality characteristic of all baroque concerto writing, and the use of a large organ would have undoubtedly disturbed this.

The two most conspicuous features of the concertos are the virtuoso style generally in evidence, together with the important element of improvisation. Sir John Hawkins tells us that Handel introduced each concerto with an improvised prelude; and several of the concertos require an improvised movement. Many editions provide 'compositions' which are inadequate in both style and content; this particular aspect of performance practice will certainly justify the study of improvisation on pastiche lines, advocated in Part Four of this book.

There are many editions of these works, some of which inflate Handel's usual two-part textures with the addition of pedal parts and the filling up of chords. This treatment of the solo part leads to an approach to the concertos which is certainly logical and consistent when a large symphony orchestra is used, but it should not be necessary to stress how false to the true nature of the works such a distortion is. Strong colouristic contrasts and variety of texture in the organ parts appear not to have interested Handel greatly, and a sparkling and lively tutti for the fast movements, contrasted with Diapasons and Flutes for the slow and softer movements seem to be what he had in mind. We have noticed previously his dislike of half-stops.

It is inescapable that these concertos should be a natural

first choice for the comparatively rare occasions when an organ and orchestra can be combined. But a successful presentation depends so much on perfect balance and rhythmical co-ordination between the two elements that a close proximity between a small body of instruments and the organ is absolutely essential. A recreation of the original conditions, with the soloist directing from a strategically placed chamber organ, is by far the best solution to the problem.

Haydn and Mozart

From the Renaissance to the classical period the idioms of the chamber organ and the harpsichord were interchangeable to a large extent, depending on the use of sustained textures. The three Haydn *Concertos per l'Organo* are delightful divertimento works, in which the usual church sonata forces of two violins, bass and keyboard may be enriched (presumably authentically) by two trumpets and timpani and a concertante treatment of the keyboard part.

The more harmonically based language of the keyboard writing is naturally fuller than that of Handel, and can easily be related to the 'clock' pieces by Haydn. Delicacy and precision of touch is needed here just as much as in the Handel concertos, but these works surely deserve to be better known, indeniably slight though they are.

The church sonatas of Mozart have already been mentioned. K.V.67 and K.V.278 are continuo pieces, but K.V.321 uses the organ both independently and also for wind-band-like harmonic support. K.V.336 includes a solo organ part in true concerto style as well as an *organo ripieno* with the violins and bass. Both works are well suited for concert use.

We have already noted the reluctance of the baroque and classical composers to combine a large organ with orchestra, and this uncertain relationship was to continue throughout the nineteenth century, with organ and orchestra competing for supremacy in size and power instead of being able to enjoy the complementary partnership possible with the chamber music approach of the previous centuries.

The romantics still saw the organ as having the dual role of earlier periods – as background and as having a certain limited solo function – but it also began to acquire a more sensational value: its tutti was now heard in some spatial relationship to the orchestra (as in the Berlioz *Te Deum*, for example); or for dramatic religio-apotheosis effects (the coda of Liszt's *A Faust Symphony*, and Mahler's Symphony No. 8). These are operatically influenced transcendental choral movements in which the text perhaps justifies the means; but the same apparatus is rather more questionable when applied to purely orchestral works such as Saint-Saëns's Symphony No. 3 or Strauss's tone poem *Also sprach Zarathustra*.

Saint-Saëns and Strauss

The nineteenth century quickly identified two aspects of its aesthetic that it thought the organ could delineate supremely well – the sentimental and the bombastic. These organ parts are usually purely harmonic in texture and are normally unconcerned with any aspect of virtuosity or technical difficulties of any kind, save that of precise coordination with the orchestra – an important enough consideration to be sure.

The Saint-Saëns Third Symphony convincingly demonstrates how well the composer, organist at St Merry in Paris for many years, calculated the sonority of the Cavaillé-Coll organ against his orchestral scoring. The transparent brilliancy and attack characteristic of this type of instrument, when the composer's dynamic markings of *forte* and *fortissimo* are scrupulously observed, produces an overwhelming effect, quite out of proportion to the musical content. But a performance in the Royal Albert Hall stays in my mind, when the coarse and opaque tutti of that organ was unleashed at its first entry in the finale – Saint-Saëns marks this *forte* only – thereby nullifying the best efforts of the orchestra to be audible at all. The French orchestral musician playing the solo part and the conductor should have known better.

The same 'King of Instruments' approach is used by Strauss in *Also sprach Zarathustra*, and the first entry of the organ tutti here, similar in effect to the Saint-Saëns, frequently reveals one basic incompatibility between the romantic organ and the symphony orchestra: tuning. The orchestral players, striving to scale the heights of Strauss's first climax, have usually sharpened by the time the cold, unyielding organ tone enters, thereby diminishing rather than enhancing the composer's intention.

Elgar and Walton

The use of the instrument as a sonorous background of an optional nature is well exemplified in Elgar's work, as is only to be expected with a composer with a West Country cathedral ambience. The conclusion of the first *Pomp and Circumstance March* and of the *'Enigma' Variations* are two of the most telling; this tradition was followed by William Walton (1902–1983) in *Crown Imperial* and *Belshazzar's Feast*.

The French, with their long and very firmly based organ culture, have shown the most persistent interest in combining organ and orchestra. Guilmant scored his first organ sonata as a Symphony for Organ and Orchestra and this genre was taken up by Widor and Dupré. The craftsmanship of their work is never in question, but the musical content is frequently too arid to interest musicians outside the organ world.

The German counterpart to Guilmant was Josef Rheinberger (1839–1901), and his Concerto in F, scored for the interesting combination of organ, three horns and strings, possesses the same engaging tunefulness, square phrasing and ultimately unmemorable quality of invention as his French colleague.

Poulenc

The first modern concerto to establish itself firmly in the repertoire was Poulenc's, for organ, strings and timpani. This imaginative piece succeeds for many reasons, the most important being the sound-world: the essential incompatibility of the forces used is exploited with such resourcefulness, the sensuous shimmer of the strings, in apposition to the very different tone of the organ, with the use of a language half-way between the classical and the romantic; all this engenders a genuine *frisson* in the listener.

As is usual with this composer, the eclecticism of the organ style is matched by the variety of the compositional idioms: German and French baroque idioms rub shoulders with Viennese classicism and Ravel quite naturally, and the moods of religious grave and worldly gay are effortlessly juxtaposed and integrated. The uninhibited secularity of parts of this concerto are apt to startle, until it is remembered how this strain runs through French organ music from Couperin to Louis Lefébure-Wély (1817–1869), and is certainly present in such pieces as the Franck Final in B flat and the Widor and Vierne symphonic finales. Poulenc wisely left the registration of the organ part to Duruflé, and his recording of the work at his church of St Etienne du Mont is a monument of modern authentic performance practice.

Poulenc's notable success with this splendid work has inspired several other composers to write for the same intriguing scoring. Leighton's concerto reveals the everpotent influence of Béla Bartók (1881–1945), notably in the closing *Chorale and Variations* movement. My own concerto was written in the same year (1969) and follows Poulenc's example in the blending of classical and romantic influences. Jean Langlais (b.1907) and Guillou have each contributed to this medium. The usefulness of this type of piece in concerts including some pre-nineteenth-century works for organ and orchestra should not be lost on impresarios.

Hindemith

It should not be forgotten that the Hindemith sonatas were predated by his Chamber Concerto for Organ of 1928 and it was inevitable that he should be asked to write a full-scale concerto. This he did for the inauguration of the new organ in the Philharmonic Hall, New York, in 1963, with Anton Heiller as soloist.

The work poses the expected problems of balance and scale. Just as the sonatas suggest the chamber style of the baroque and early classical periods, so the organ writing here is suggestive of the same approach. Although much of the orchestral writing stresses the delicate and subtle, rather than the rhetorical, there is still an inherent imbalance between a classical organ and the full romantic symphony orchestra, however restrained its use. Heiller's own concerto is in a similar vein and cannot be regarded as having solved the difficulty.

A neo-classical language, as opposed to the classical spirit, is now outworn, and the earnest, craftsmanlike marriage of this with such a colouristically based ensemble as the modern symphony orchestra is almost bound to lead to an uncomfortable result. A fresh and original approach is needed for the combination of organ and orchestra.

Organ concertos with full orchestra remain a rarity and the inherent unease of the combination must be an important factor. It is not without significance that Messiaen, equally at home with organ and orchestra, has not attempted to combine them.

The combination of organ and brass band is an almost unexplored medium but I have made a start with the symphonic suite *The Fenlands*. The at first sight unlikely combination does work remarkably well.

The use of the organ with single or small groups of instruments implies a chamber music approach which admits of less compromise than the orchestral concerto. Trumpet or cornet and organ make an obvious duo, with plenty of baroque material for transcription, and a few modern works. A much more intimate partnership is needed for the *Sonata da Chiesa* for flute and organ by Frank Martin (1890–1974), but this is a transcription from the original for flute and string orchestra.

Organ and piano has possibilities – Liszt should have done something in this field – as has organ and violin, and Karg-Elert's experiments with these ideas are of considerable interest. His many collections of *Chorale-Improvisations* include several works involving other instruments. An effective, if fairly obvious example, is the inclusion of brass quartet and timpani in *Wunderbarer König* from Op. 65; but *Vom Himmel hoch*, Op. 78, and *Nun ruhen alle Wälder*, Op. 87, introduce a chorus of treble voices and a solo violin to more poetic effect. This last, the third of a set of Three Symphonic Chorales, is perhaps the last word on the romantic era's vision of the Protestant chorale.

It was published in 1911; the harmonic language is appropriately Mahlerian and even uses an occasional glissando in the string-like texture of the polyphony. But would it sound better on the orchestra? It would, but the music is not as good as Mahler, and here we are brought up forcibly yet again by the frequent and fatal defect of the work of so many romantic organ composers. Their music would sound better if scored for orchestra rather than organ, but the quality is such that it would not survive in the concert hall on its musical merits.

The organ has improbably been paired with the 'soft Guitarr' to point, no doubt, a useful contrast between Brady's 'Wanton heat and loose Desire' and 'Seraphic Flame and Heav'nly Love', but as yet only in transcriptions of material by Bach.

Nineteen
Organ Transcription

Just as the description 'orchestral organ' tends to make the
early music devotee bridle – the organ has always been
largely based upon the instrumental ensemble of whatever
period in its history – so the term 'orchestral transcription'
arouses similar outrage. But, as we have seen, the earliest
organ music was a transcription of vocal material, and this
practice continued throughout the succeeding centuries:
the sixteenth-century Mulliner Book, viol accompaniments by Gibbons and others arranged for organ, the
arrangement for solo keyboard of concertos by Vivaldi,
Handel and others.

Bach was an inveterate transcriber. Even if the authenticity of some of his arrangements is questionable, at least
two of the concertos from Vivaldi (BWV 593 and
BWV 596) are accepted, and there is no doubt about the
'Schübler' Preludes, five of which are untransposed
arrangements of cantata movements. Bach's writing for
organ is often so dependent on string idioms that we ought
not to be in the least surprised that he should bodily
transfer movements from one medium to another. Trans-
ference of idiom was, after all, one of the main stylistic
features of the baroque era, and figurations that were
shared by voices, wind, strings, and organ were common
property.

The trio sonatas are examples of pieces that stand
halfway between string-influenced organ music such as the
G major Prelude and Fugue (BWV 541) and arrangements
such as the 'Schübler' Preludes. The single Trio Movement

in D minor (BWV 1027A) is probably an arrangement from an instrumental trio sonata, and at least two movements from the six trio sonatas were transcriptions of instrumental pieces.

We may well ask – in the light of Bach's example – what a 'truly idiomatic organ style' is. The eighteenth century was, of course, a much less 'historically conscious' age than our own, but one very much concerned with the usefulness and practicality of its music. The Handel organ concertos are a good example of this. Written for the composer to play himself, with the orchestral forces assembled for his oratorio performances, what could be more natural than that the publisher Walsh should, in 1738, issue a version of the solo keyboard part with the orchestral sections transcribed for the unaccompanied organist? The set of transcriptions of the opus 4 concertos was issued with the composer's permission and has recently been made available in a modern edition.

The Handel concertos, generally speaking, are so much more attractive than his voluntaries that organists have wanted to include them in their programmes. As a result, very many nineteenth- and twentieth-century versions have appeared, including those by William Best, Dupré and Helmut Walcha. Most have thought it necessary to add pedal parts and to fill out the harmonies of the solo part. But the eighteenth century had a better understanding of what was right in the keyboard transcription of orchestral textures, and it is to be hoped that the Walsh publications will be carefully studied and used.

So successful was the opus 4 set that Walsh brought out another set of six transcriptions two years later. Only the first two of these were in fact organ concertos (the first was the well-known F major *The Cuckoo and the Nightingale*); the others were transcriptions of four of the opus 6 string concertos. These should certainly be made available in a modern edition. The organ is not so rich in solo music by Handel that Walsh's publication can be dismissed as 'mere arranger's hack work'.

The pieces by Mozart and Haydn for mechanical organ are of course transcriptions, and how poor the repertoire would be without them! The Haydn concertos and the most interesting of Mozart's church sonatas, in suitably idiomatic arrangements, might be well received by contemporary audiences. Organists need encouragement to make their own versions of this material. As much useful insight into Mozart and the organ would be gained by a twentieth-century organist at work on a church sonata transcription, as Bach no doubt gained from his Vivaldi arrangements.

Mendelssohn did not concern himself with transcriptions for any instrument, but in the slow movements from his sonatas we can see his *Songs without Words* piano idiom adapted for the organ. The *Allegretto* from the Fourth Sonata is a good example of a style for which there existed no precedent in previous organ music.

The Schumann sketches, studies and fugues are examples of piano writing that needs thoughtful adaptation to the organ, in spite of the inclusion of a pedal part. The significance of these pieces for the newly emerging piano-based organ idiom can hardly be over-estimated.

Of all nineteenth-century transcribers for the organ Liszt was unquestionably the most indefatigable. Of the forty-seven organ pieces, all, except the first, *Ad nos, ad salutarem undam* (an operatic paraphrase?), may be regarded as transcriptions of his own or other composers' material. They range from Roland de Lassus (1532–1594) to his contemporaries, and include piano, choral and orchestral pieces.

The dividing line between the classical and the romantic view of the organ may be more aptly drawn with these works of Schumann and Liszt than with the closing eighteenth-century decadence typified by Georg Joseph Vogler (1749–1814). Liszt was no more concerned with respecting the 'essential nature' of the organ in his transcriptions than he was with respecting the 'essential nature' of the piano in his versions of Berlioz and Wagner. Much of this material is slight but there are a few gems.

Why are Liszt's organ and harmonium transcriptions generally of poorer quality than his piano versions of, say, Schubert's songs? Why does the romantic organ so often bring out the more feeble aspects of a composer's work? First, there is always the temptation to deal in the sentimental religiosity of liturgical 'sweet nothings' which the Celestes, Tremulants and soft 32′ stops provide so easily. Then, there is the amateur element which has always been an important force in the organ and church-music confraternity. Technical ease and spiritual atmospherics easily combine to debase the stern discipline of great organ art, and Liszt is not free from blame in many of his transcriptions.

The more demanding Bach and Wagner pieces are of interest as object lessons in the techniques of transcription employed by Liszt. It is noticeable that Bach comes off much more naturally than Wagner. Orchestral music relies so heavily on expressive nuance, and sensuousness of sound will not translate as easily as music of limited and stable sound, with line and counterpoint as its structural basis. Despite this, Wagner was the composer on which most organists set their sights. Sighs of agony and ecstasy simply had to be made available to the newly evolved imitation romantic orchestra – even the *Liebestod* from *Tristan und Isolde*. Strangely enough, more obviously suitable things, such as the *Good Friday Music* from *Parsifal* and the Prelude to Act III of *Die Meistersinger*, were neglected. The *Ride of the Valkyries* was a clear must. This does, indeed, come off very well, but it is basically a French toccata, swirling figuration, Pedal reeds and all.

The work of Edwin Lemare (1865–1934) in this field set a standard hardly to be surpassed, and he readily turned his attention to Elgar's many orchestral marches, pointing up yet again the orchestral nature of Elgar's organ writing in the Sonata in G. Elgar did, of course, pay back his debt to the orchestral organ with his fascinating transcription for orchestra of the Bach Fantasia and Fugue in C minor (BWV 537).

Organ

The organ transcription of orchestral music was especially popular in the English town hall recital series before the development of radio and gramophone recording enabled people to hear the repertoire in its original form. With this excuse removed and the growing revival of interest in the pre-nineteenth-century organ aesthetic, in both the instrument and its repertoire, the transcription quickly fell from favour and it became almost disreputable to include a transcription in a recital. Where 'authenticity' was the new watchword, how could transcriptions be justified?

As transcriptions fell from favour, the mass audience the organ had enjoyed in the nineteenth century declined. Today the usual 'small' audience for a recital will contain mainly organists and other initiated enthusiasts. But this exclusive attitude has now largely been worked through, and transcriptions are beginning to reappear in programmes.

Much baroque music for any medium will transcribe well for the organ, but as there is already so much original material already available, interest is bound to centre on later keyboard music, especially where the colouristic range of the organ appears to offer possibilities not found in the original medium.

An outstanding example of such a work is *Pictures at an Exhibition* by Modest Mussorgsky (1839–1881). This often orchestrated work is equally effective as an organ piece. The keyboard basis of the original is retained, but the organ offers a wide range of appropriate colours as well as the sustained tone that many of the movements require. In addition, the organ sound has a directness and starkness that seems entirely right for this often earthy music.

What kind of music is most suitable for transcription, bearing in mind that the new instruments will increasingly tend towards classical principles and repertoire? The first point is that works must be chosen that depend more on line and consistency of texture than on sonority and kaleidoscopic changes of colour for their effect. Over-frequent piston pushing will not be appropriate or available for the new transcriptions; Ravel rather than Debussy will suit our new-old organs; neo-classicism rather than impressionism. The single 'affection' of the baroque rather than the dramatic dualism of the classical period will best suit 'museum' instruments. This, of course, is why Mussorgsky works so well. When solo effects are required we shall turn more to the mutations than the orchestral imitative ranks to be found on the Solo division of the romantic organ.

Bach transcriptions today may seem misconceived. After all, is there not an abundance of Bach organ music, much of which is not often heard except in 'complete' series, or integral recording projects? But if we reflect on the important part transcription played in Bach's life; we may perhaps even regard the act of transcription as part of the new 'authenticity'. Indeed, as we strive to emulate the phrasings, bowings and articulation on our instruments, the transcription of movements from the solo partitas and orchestral suites may be a most useful exercise in understanding Bach's organ idiom.

Whereas the older generation of transcribers freely transferred Bach's original version to a romantic or modern idiom, we can try to see our transcriptions through the eyes of Bach, and use his own techniques of transcription as our guide. For instance, in the light of those cantata movements that he transcribed without continuo filling as trio movements – *Wachet auf*, for instance – why should we not try *Jesu, joy of man's desiring* in the same way? After all, Bach's lively oboe obbligato will transfer to a Nazard or Tierce combination much more readily than to a romanticized piano version.

There would be many opportunities to experiment with period registration: *Sanctify us by thy goodness* as a trio, for instance, with the tune on a Pedal Trompet and the bass and treble on contrasted manuals. The *Chaconne* from the Partita in D minor for solo violin would make a most stimulating exercise in the comprehension of the relationship between baroque string techniques and organ idioms. Far from apologizing for the fresh interest in Bach transcription, we should welcome it as a most stimulating exercise in creative Bach study and interpretation.

Elgar is another composer who has frequently engaged the attention of transcribers. One of the most interesting of his works in this respect is the Organ Sonata No. 2 in B flat, Op. 87A. This was transcribed from the *Severn Suite* for Brass Band (1930) by Ivor Atkins in 1933. Much of Atkins's work is good, but he incomprehensibly omits the *Minuet* and inserts a feeble cadenza in its place between the *Fugue* and the *Coda*. A new version of this Second Sonata is long overdue and would lead to a re-assessment of this neglected work for organ. Elgar's band textures certainly transfer well to the organ, and make available to the repertoire a most valuable work.

The 'historical' approach to the organ today by no means rules out the art of transcription. On the contrary, it positively encourages it, both for its educative function, for both audience and player, and for the healthy contact it gives with the wider world of music. The organist has always been suspected of an unwillingness to step outside the organ loft, and the presentday trend of specialization in 'early' music may seem to reinforce the organist's isolation. Thoughtful work at transcription techniques will serve as a useful corrective. The words of Dmitry Shostakovich apply with equal force to the art of transcription as they do to the art of orchestration: 'Nothing compares with the feeling you get when orchestrating a revered composer. I think it's the ideal method for studying a work, and I would recommend that all young composers make their own versions of the works of those masters from whom they want to learn. I had known *Boris* [*Godunov*] almost by heart since my Conservatoire days, but it was only when I orchestrated it that I sensed and experienced it as if it were my own work.'

Twenty
Organ Accompaniment

Although interest in the organ as a solo instrument has increased to a striking extent since the Second World War, it is still true to say that most organ appointments are concerned more with the instrument as an ensemble medium, mostly with voices, either choral or massed, than with its solo role.

Church appointments greatly outnumber secular ones. The function of the organ in church liturgies has always been of prime importance, and much of its solo repertoire (some would say the finest part) has sprung from its liturgical involvement. It is by no means easy to determine with any certainty how this first developed. The fact that the early organs were placed near the choir, so that they could participate in the sung portions of the service, either doubling, decorating or in alternation, makes it clear that the accompanimental function of the instrument took precedence over its independent solo role.

The development of the solo function of the instrument occurs as late as the seventeenth century, when the west wall was increasingly favoured as the most appropriate site for the organ. The many transcriptions of motets and anthems from the thirteenth to sixteenth centuries, together with the surviving organ books which contain skeleton versions of choral music (often the only source of some pieces), make it clear that the supporting role of the organ existed from its earliest appearance in churches and cathedrals.

What of the plainsong era? The function of the organ in

171

Organ

the performance of plainchant is one of the most fascinating topics in the history of music, and it remains a vexing problem to this day. Was it accompanied? And should it be accompanied today? The Portative Organ would almost certainly have given the pitch, and reminded the singers of the melody to be sung – as today. It may have duplicated the chant with some form of decoration, either horizontal

Organ accompaniment for A solis ortus cardine (Mode III)

or vertical (organum), or it may have reinforced the tenor voice in cantus firmus pieces.

The rhythmic interpretation of the chant is still a matter for conjecture, but most scholars agree that it needs to flow easily. The duplication of the melody in the organ part is unhelpful in this respect, but a style of harmony using only the notes of the mode, and coinciding with the natural stresses of the text, seems to be the most appropriate system for today, with either a Latin or a vernacular text. My example has an English text: the Vespers Office Hymn for Christmas Day. The best stop to use for this harmonic background to the voices would be a mellow 8′ Flute.

We can be sure that choirmasters of all periods have used the organ as a background support as needed. In England there are many organ books giving such parts. These choral outlines were decorated according to the skill and taste of the player, and if the organ is used in a Jacobean Service today the accompaniment should not be restricted to a mere routine duplication of the vocal line. In any case, independent parts for the organ were soon developed, Byrd's Verse (Second) Service being an early and beautiful example.

Many early seventeenth-century pieces were scored for viol consort, but an organ sketch was also usually included, and this may be ornamented and amplified by such material from the viol parts as the player can effectively manage. A chamber organ of a few ranks is the best instrument to use for such pieces, and sufficient tonal variety can be obtained from the contrast and combination of 8′ alone, 8′ and 4′, and 8′ and 2′, according to the solo/chorus textures used and the character of the work.

The elaboration and decoration of a skeleton vocal score leads naturally on to continuo realization. This is one of the most interesting fields for a display of musicianship. The shorthand of a figured or unfigured bass line presents a unique challenge to the creative powers of an accompanist-improviser, and, indeed, to his sense of historical style.

Most modern editions of Renaissance and baroque

music provide fully notated realizations of the original organ bass. However useful these may be to those accompanists who lack either the interest or the skill to invent their own realizations, these editions do lead to a stereotyped and unthinking acceptance of a version that should be variable and spontaneous in execution. There is immense satisfaction to be derived from this work, as it enables the organist to enter into a working partnership with the composer.

The transcription of the viol parts in Jacobean music has already been mentioned; the same practice applies to the string textures of Blow, Purcell and Bach, and such work can be very demanding. The apt rendering of string idioms on the organ in works of this period demands much thought and practice. It is here that work on baroque transcription techniques will prove to be of the greatest benefit. The important thing here is to distinguish between the essential and the less essential in the texture. Here again the use of a modern edition may save time and labour, but it will not yield such rewards as the use of a full score.

The problems increase with classical and romantic works. If a reduced score is used, the player should at least go through it with a full score, marking any changes he considers will improve the effect, and deciding on effective registrational translations of the original scoring. The late nineteenth-century English cathedral and town hall organ now comes naturally into its own, having at least partially evolved in response to the demands of large choral society accompanimental duties.

Along with this use of material from oratorios and cantatas in the nineteenth century appeared the first use of carefully indicated independent organ accompaniments. In England, this new development was led by S. S. Wesley, and it is not overstating the case to say that subsequent developments in English church music depend almost entirely on his pioneering work.

Such textures as those found in 'Blessed be the God and Father', for example, lie behind the work of Stanford and

Edward Bairstow (1874–1946), and in their imaginative detail remain unsurpassed over a hundred years later. Organ management is a vital element in the performance of this kind of accompaniment; rhythmic control, unimpaired by changes of registration, is of the essence.

Today it is quite common for choir direction and accompaniment to be in the hands of separate musicians, often aided by the use of closed-circuit television. This is by far the best arrangement, as the conductor can supervise every detail of the performance, including the setting of the initial tempo, the adjustment of balance between organ and choir – often very difficult for the player to judge – and generally control the overall conception of the piece. This should include points of colour in the registration, and the direction of introductions, interludes and postludes.

The usefulness of this is often questioned, but, as well as continuity of overall control, the concentration of all the performers is maintained, and the requisite discipline of the choir 'singing through their rests' can more easily be secured. It is an equally useful discipline for an organist to learn to follow the beat of another musician.

Organists tend to be the most wayward of performers because of their lofty remoteness – usually better for mystique than music. Nevertheless, the separation of conductor and accompanist is a fairly recent innovation in churches, and one not universally welcomed. It is still not uncommon for organists to exercise both functions with variable success from a console that is in reasonably close proximity to the singers.

Both singing and playing are apt to suffer from this method of performance, but it is at least an improvement on an older procedure, whereby the organist, unseen by the choir, needed to give a preliminary 'thump' before every choral entry. This irritating call to attention became a standard feature of much nineteenth-century English cathedral music. It occurs frequently in Stainer, for instance, and sometimes mars the work of as good a composer as S. S. Wesley. It is even residually present in

Organ

Vaughan Williams's fine tune *Sine Nomine*.

Vaughan Williams: Sine Nomine

In fact, organ, choir and congregation can learn to synchronize their starts, and thereby immeasurably improve the vitality and precision of their work. This 'remote control' of the choir led inevitably to an over-loud accompaniment, as a result of the organist's effort to make his intentions clear, as well as to the use of over-phrasing and rigid tempi in order to secure the maximum possible cohesion. None of the desirable virtues of a good accompaniment style – good balance, delicate phrasing and precise but subtle co-ordination – were likely to be achieved with this system.

The sensitivity of a really good accompanist is more rarely found than that of a good soloist and is a much more socially useful accomplishment. It deserves to be studied far more seriously than it usually is, and accompaniment practice, with the aid of a local choir, could be advantageously exchanged for solo practice time. The essence of good accompaniment lies in the integration of one musical personality with another, and the highest summation is to be found in the twin peaks of continuo realization, and the execution of some modern works.

Two of Stanford's *Magnificat* settings, those in G and A major, are outstanding examples of independent organ accompaniments. The G major is a most delicate evocation of a young girl at a spinning wheel – the influence of the German romantic school on Stanford could hardly be more clearly revealed than here – and a successful performance needs the expressive control of a Schubert song.

Similarly, the influence of Brahms (the Second Symphony, perhaps?) hangs heavily over the A major setting. The orchestral conception of the organ writing is obvious from the outset, and it is no surprise to learn that it is a transcription from an orchestral version prepared for a Three Choirs Festival service.

Such works as this remind us how comparatively limited the organ can sound in contrast to the opulent expressiveness of nineteenth-century orchestration. Yet the organ should not be regarded as second best. Players should feel stimulated by the orchestral palette into ever finer subtleties of tone and touch, as well as to exploit that freedom that a single performer can impart to music.

Another engrossing work for the accompanist is the *Requiem* by Duruflé. The subtle blend of 'churchy' counterpoint and secular impressionism, together with the work's basis in plainchant, gives it a fascination hardly approached by any other work. Duruflé wisely tried to meet differing performance circumstances by providing three versions of the accompaniment: full orchestra; organ, strings and timpani, and organ alone. This last version has some technical difficulties, notably in the *Sanctus*, but the real problem lies in the management and integration of the fluctuating tempo changes of the large-scale sections, with the freedom which the combination of plainchant and modern harmonic idioms demands.

Liszt's *Via Crucis*, the *Missa Brevis* of Zoltán Kodály (1882–1967), and Leighton's *Crucifixus pro Nobis* are other notable examples of extended works in which the organ plays a role of crucial importance.

The accompanist needs the virtues of a good soloist: a fully developed technique, a sense of performance, and a grasp of stylistic considerations. In addition he has to acquire a sense of ensemble, together with a fully developed range of keyboard skills such as harmonization, figured-bass realization, improvisation, vocal and orchestral score-reading and transcription techniques.

Twenty-one
An Outline Course
of Instruction

At what point are pianists ready to begin organ study? They should certainly have acquired pianistic fluency, together with a sensitivity to tone and dynamics, and they should know all the major and minor scales. Continued work at the piano and/or harpsichord will be of the greatest value alongside organ study. Equally it is of the utmost importance that students should be trained in the techniques of harmony, counterpoint and composition, pastiche or original, both on paper and (even more important) at the keyboard. The study of improvisation should be linked to the individual student's progress in technique and repertoire at every stage.

I set out below a suggested scheme to provide the student with a thorough knowledge of organ technique, based on an understanding of the instrument's evolution and repertoire. Purely technical exercises are kept to a minimum; this outline course is more concerned with indicating a logical and palatable sequence of pieces and ideas taken from the various historical periods discussed in the book. It will be necessary for the student to refer back to the relevant chapter as required.

An Introduction to the Instrument

The first lesson should include a general introduction to the instrument; the pitch and tone quality of the stops; the relationship of manuals and pedals. A comparison with other instruments will offer useful insight into touch and phrasing: piano, harpsichord, string and wind instruments should be related to the organ. With these points demonstrated and discussed, the pupil can sit on the bench and begin to get the 'feel' of the instrument.

Good posture is best ensured by asking the pupil to raise his arms above his head as high as possible, and then hold his body in the same position as he brings his arms down to the keyboards. (This posture habit can be encouraged by practising pedal exercises with the arms raised, a procedure well worth maintaining throughout a career). The bench should be adjusted so that the player's feet are just touching the pedals, as close to the short keys as possible. Modern pedal boards offer a wide range of available position, so that the feet can pass easily behind each other. Older boards did not, and the playing technique was based mainly on the toes. If possible, the initial lessons should be taken on a small and responsive mechanical-action instrument. A large cathedral organ is the least suitable instrument for the early stages of instruction.

The pupil can now begin to play isolated notes, chords and scales with various registrations. With separate notes he will be introduced to the basic principle of all performance: the most careful listening to every sound and the most acute awareness of every sound produced. In particular, the varying speeds of the opening and closing of the pallet, and the related digital feel, should be experienced at the first lesson and practised with hands separately in slow scales played perfectly legato. This should be followed by scales using the 'clear' legato touch – best illustrated by playing the scale with a single finger, endeavouring to keep as smooth a line as possible. When the difference between legato and 'clear' legato is understood, then staccato, based on three-quarters and one-half of the notated values, may be introduced.

All this work can then be applied to the pedals, using separate notes and scales of up to two sharps and two flats, with alternate toes. The use of the heels should be introduced with slow trills on short and long keys in the middle of the board, using the same touches. (The need for a loose and relaxed ankle will be at once apparent.) When mastered using the middle of the pedal board, this simple exercise should be practised with each foot in every position over the board, so introducing the occasional necessity of pivoting the body. Modern instruments, with their large pedal boards, have encouraged the use of pivoting; it need rarely be used on old instruments, or historical copies. Nevertheless it is a technique the student should be aware of from the outset of his training.

Finally, scales in different rhythms, together with a variety of slurring and accentuation, should be practised on both manuals and pedals.

All this work will take up a great deal of time in the first lessons, but the point of this guide to the organ is to suggest a course of study through actual music, so we must now consider a possible first-year scheme, together with suggestions for the repertoire to be studied in two following years and after. The first year should certainly include frequent revision of the technical exercises already begun, with much attention to their relationships to the music being studied.

First Year

First Term

Manuals Alone

  Robertsbridge Codex
  Buxheimer Orgelbüch
  Mulliner Book (complete or abridged edition)
  Sweelinck: Fantasias

Manuals and Pedals

Titelouze: *Twelve Hymns of the Church*
Mendelssohn: Sonatas
Vierne: Préambule, Berceuse, Rêverie (*Twenty-four Pieces in Free Style*)

This method of tuition involves the acquisition of a number of large and fairly expensive complete editions, but since these are the basis of an organist's library it seems a good idea to get these from the outset, rather than piecemeal and inevitably duplicated in anthologies and tutors. It leads the student to appreciate a composer's work as a whole, ensuring a comprehension of range and style that a few isolated movements certainly cannot give and it should also encourage him to sight-read regularly, as his technique progresses, rather than to develop the more usual obsession with set pieces. Good sight-reading is the foundation of keyboard musicianship (transposition and score-reading, for instance) and students need constantly to be reminded of its importance.

The scheme of work I have suggested for the first term brings the pupil into contact with two centuries of early organ music, the heart of the repertoire; with the romantic transition to a lyrical, piano-influenced idiom; and then on to the early twentieth century, with use of the swell box and the idea of organ management generally. Some of the slow movements from the sonatas will be the best introduction to Mendelssohn.

Along with all this work, if the student is ready for it, should go work on the first exercises in improvisation (see next chapter). The student will notice the connection between these and the Titelouze style, and so his understanding through interpretation will go hand in hand with his understanding through creativity.

Organ

Second Term
The second term's work will continue to revise and refine the pieces already learned, with the addition of the following:

Manuals Alone

Frescobaldi: *Fiori musicali* (1635)
Couperin: Two Organ Masses
Scheidt: *Tabulatura nova* (1624)

Manuals and Pedals
The Couperin and Scheidt collections mentioned above contain pieces that continue the use of pedals in cantus firmus textures; they also introduce the use of the pedals as a supporting harmonic bass. The chorale preludes of Buxtehude may then be introduced. They contain pedal parts of an independent melodic character in a simple contrapuntal texture. For romantic work the Schumann Sketches or Brahms chorale preludes would be appropriate. Modern pieces could include the *Choral Dorien* of Alain and the Psalm Prelude, Op. 32 No. 2, by Howells.

Work on improvisation would continue with the plainchant cantus firmus style and the beginnings of simple chorale prelude treatments could be introduced.

Third Term
The third term would expand the repertoire from the volumes already in use, and could be supplemented with some of the short chorale preludes by Bach from the miscellaneous collections and the *Orgelbüchlein*. The *Cantabile* of Franck and *Le Banquet céleste* of Messiaen could be introduced to further the student's knowledge of nineteenth- and twentieth-century music. If the student is ready, the work on improvisation could go on to free style of the English eighteenth century.

This outline of a first year's work may be thought unduly ambitious by some. It is of course only a guide, giving a wide choice of material, and is quite realistic for a serious student who wishes to work intensively. Taken at a more moderate pace, the work can be spaced out and diluted to suit those of a less strenuous disposition and ambition.

Second Year

First Term

Bach: Prelude and Fugue in E minor (BWV 533)
Bach: Prelude and Fugue in C (BWV 545)
Bach: Alla Breve (BWV 549)
Bach: Fantasia in G (BWV 572)
Bach: Fantasia in C minor (BWV 562)
Buxtehude: Chaconne in E minor
Buxtehude: Chorale Preludes
Clérambault: Two Suites
Purcell: Voluntary in G
Mendelssohn: Sonata No. 2
Vaughan Williams: Rhosymedre (*Three Preludes on Welsh Hymn Tunes*)
Elgar: *Andante espressivo* (Sonata in G, Op. 28)

Improvisation: Short contrapuntal structures

Second Term

Bach: Toccata and Fugue in D minor (BWV 565)
Bach: Trio Sonata No. 1 (BWV 525)
Bach: *Orgelbüchlein*
Bach: Fantasia and Fugue in C minor (BWV 537)
Buxtehude: Prelude, Fugue and Ciacona
Buxtehude: Passcaglia in D minor
de Grigny: *Veni Creator* (complete)
de Grigny: *Messe* (selected movements)
Purcell: Voluntary for a Double Organ
Mendelssohn: Sonata No. 5

Organ

Franck: *Pièce Héroïque*
Messiaen: *L'Eglise éternelle*

Improvisation: Binary, ternary and rondo forms

Third Term

Bach: Passacaglia and Fugue in C minor (BWV 582)
Bach: Trio Sonata No. 2 (BWV 526)
Bach: Prelude and Fugue in A minor (BWV 543)
Buxtehude: Prelude and Fugue in G minor
Franck: Choral in A minor
Liszt: Variations on 'Weinen, Klagen, Sorgen, Zagen'
Vierne: *Symphonie II* (selected movements)
Elgar: *Allegro maestoso* (Sonata in G, Op. 28)

Third Year

First Term

Bach: Trio Sonata No. 3 (BWV 527)
Bach: Prelude and Fugue in C minor (BWV 546)
Bach: Prelude and Fugue in E flat (BWV 552)
de Grigny: *Messe*
du Mage: *Livre d'orgue*
Franck: Choral in B minor
Mendelssohn: Sonata No. 1
Liszt: Fantasia and Fugue on BACH
Messiaen: *La Nativité* (selected movements)

Improvisation: Fugal treatments

Second Term

Bach: Fantasia and Fugue in G minor (BWV 542)
Bach: Prelude and Fugue in E minor (BWV 548)
Bach: Eighteen Chorale Preludes
Bach: Trio Sonata No. 4 (BWV 528)
Mozart: Fantasia in F minor (K.V.594)

Franck: Final in B flat
Reger: Benedictus
Reger: Introduction and Passacaglia in D minor
Widor: *Symphonie VI*
Vierne: *Symphonie III*
Wills: *Tongues of Fire*

Improvisation: Ground bass and variations

Third Term

Bach: *Klavierübung* No. 3
Bach: Prelude and Fugue in B minor (BWV 544)
Bach: Trio Sonata No. 5 (BWV 529)
Bach: Trio Sonata No. 6 (BWV 530)
Mozart: Fantasia in F minor (K.V.608)
Mendelssohn: Prelude and Fugue in C minor
Franck: Choral in E
Liszt: Fantasia and Fugue on 'Ad nos, ad salutarem undam'
Widor: *Symphonie Romane*
Vierne: *Symphonie VI*
Messiaen: *Messe de la Pentecôte*
Howells: Psalm Prelude, Second Set, No. 3

Improvisation: Sonata structures

Of course the student will aid his studies by the most careful listening to good players as frequently as he can manage. The fingers and the ear should be educated with experience of organs in as many countries with a good tradition as possible, both for historic and for new work. The work of such builders as Silbermann, Schnitger, Clicquot, Cavaillé-Coll and Willis should be personally explored. Recordings do help, but beware of modelling an interpretation on one admired performance. Through travel and direct experience try to find a standard of mechanical action that will serve as a touchstone. The work of such builders as Magnussen, Anderson, Marcussen and Fisk will make a useful start to such studies.

Twenty-two
Organ Improvisation I

In England the systematic study of improvisation has been, and still is, neglected, whereas, on the Continent, it has always been included in an organist's training. Until quite recently the only organists to make a serious study of this ancient art belonged either to the Catholic tradition of France and Austria, or to the Lutheran tradition of Germany, Holland and Scandinavia.

Other instrumentalists today who play aleatoric music find that they have scope for improvisation in an ensemble. In the three centuries preceding our own we find that most of the outstanding musicians were complete all-rounders, equally engaged as composers, performers and improvisers. Bach, Mozart, Beethoven, Liszt and Bruckner were all renowned as improvisers, and we may be sure that this art was also generally practised by their less gifted contemporaries.

If improvisation is to be taken seriously, sufficient time must be allotted to its study. A few minutes at the end of an organ lesson is not adequate for this purpose. Ideally, a separate lesson each week should be given, and a daily practice session undertaken. This sustained work is usually neglected, and this neglect is the main reason for little or no progress being made by the student.

When we come to disciplined study, we need to work on the basis of competence in keyboard harmony, together with the study of harmony, counterpoint and free composition on paper. This is time consuming, but it is a commitment that is essential to progress. Just as harmony, counterpoint and composition must be studied from the finest examples of the past, so I believe that the study of improvisation is also best based on stylistic imitation.

This study will not inhibit creativity – far from it. The technical foundations acquired by the student will allow his own ideas full realization. The close study of the music of the past this entails serves to improve the student's understanding of the music, resulting in performances of increased depth and perception. So we begin our studies in improvisation having already obtained a fair competence on paper, and having achieved a reasonable facility in keyboard harmony.

The present study is based on two basic ideas. One is the use of pre-existent material – a plainchant cantus firmus or a chorale melody – and the other is the contrapuntal approach. The main weakness of much untrained improvisation is that it is a meandering succession of chords, without any sense of line, progression or shape. I believe, therefore, that the first steps should consist of simple contrapuntal work.

The idea that improvisation consists of sitting down at an instrument and expecting inspiration to descend is of course a piece of romantic nonsense. This will happen no more to the improviser than it will to the composer. There must be a basic flair, but essentially improvisation is an acquired skill – a technique that can be learned and developed. The idea that improvisation must be practised causes surprise to some people, and it is true that study cannot ensure the invention of high-quality material. With many people improvisation will always remain more or less imitative, but this is not a matter of great importance. The study of improvisation develops musicianship to a greater degree than any other aspect of training, which, quite apart from its usefulness or interest on any specific occasion, is more than adequate justification for its study.

Constant revision will be necessary if the skill is to be retained and developed. Although essential material is included here, the teacher must be responsible for providing further exercises along the same lines, as needed. The work in this chapter aims at the development of contrapuntal improvisation in two to four parts, using firstly plainchant and chorale melodies, and then more freely constructed movements based in the eighteenth-century English voluntary and French *Livre d'orgue* idioms.

Exercises Using Plainchant Melodies

The student is required to add one, two and three parts against a plainsong cantus firmus. Apart from suspensions and occasional accented passing notes, consonant intervals only should be used, the aim being to improvise a smooth, independent melodic line, with a careful mixture of similar and contrary motion. The most useful examples of this kind of movement are to be found in the *hymnes* and masses of Couperin, de Grigny, Titelouze and Frescobaldi.

This modal work, in five stages, is closely related to the old 'strict counterpoint' method of training. It has great value for improvisation, requiring considerable concentration, as it is by no means as easy as might be thought at first. It naturally inculcates the ability to think ahead essential for fluent improvisation.

Exercise 1
Add note against note to this Mode IV melody:

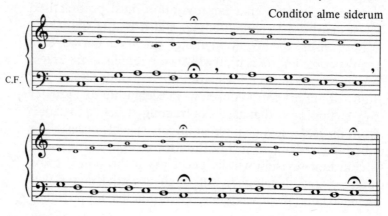

Conditor alme siderum

Exercise 2

Add two minims against each note of the cantus:

189

Exercise 3

Add four crotchets against each note of the cantus, being careful to think in phrases:

C.F.

190

Exercise 4

Add syncopated and suspended minims on the following pattern:

C.F.

* The pattern may be broken, if desirable.

191

Exercise 5

Add a part containing a mixture of all the procedures practised so far, with some use of quavers, as follows:

This work in two parts must be practised until real fluency is attained before three-part work is attempted. The student should write out his own practice material, using plainsong melodies from the *English Hymnal*.

Three-part work may now be attempted, following the same steps as for two-part work, but playing the cantus on the pedals:

Exercise 6
Complete:

Exercise 7 Complete:

Exercise 8 Complete:

194

Exercise 9 Complete:

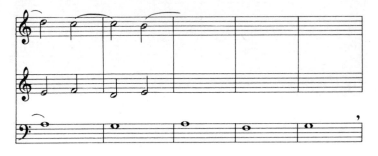

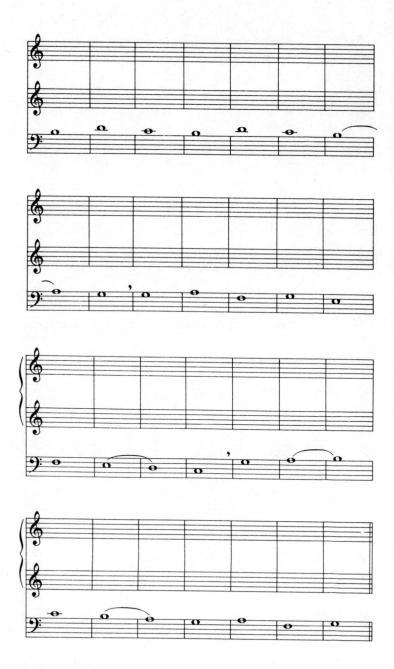

196

Exercise 10 Complete:

Organ

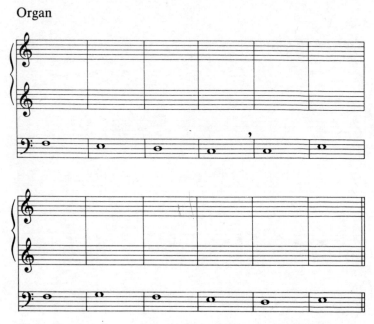

Four-part work completes this section, based on the completion of actual movements by the French seventeenth- and eighteenth-century school as follows:

Exercise 11 Continue:

Titelouze: A solis artus cardine

Exercise 12 Continue:

Couperin: Plein chant
(Messe pour les Paroisses)

Organ

Chorale and Hymn Tune Treatments

The ability to improvise on a chorale or hymn tune is a most useful skill for a church organist. A quiet opening volun-tary may be based on a melody to be sung later in the service. A long processional hymn gains immensely from the insertion of organ interludes based on the tune. During the communion of the choir a prelude based on the following hymn is appropriate, and the extension of the conclusion of a hymn – from a couple of lines to cover the completion of the collection to an extended postlude at the end of the service – is often needed. The chorale preludes of Buxtehude and Bach are models to be studied and analysed here. Bach used all the techniques of his time, and his works in this genre are an inexhaustible source of interest and instruction.

Before work on the exercises is begun a most useful preparatory exercise is to play the melody of any chosen hymn on the pedals and to harmonize it in as many convinc-ing ways as possible. In this work the top line should provide a counter-melody of character and interest. All the modulatory possibilities should be explored. The exercises using plainchant melodies will have been of great prepara-tory value for the exercises in this section.

Beginning with two-part writing on the manuals, then with left hand and pedals, this part of the work concludes with the tune played on the pedals in cantus firmus style with two parts above. In Exercise 16 the decoration of the tune into a more elaborate melodic line, with accompany-ing parts on a second manual and pedals, is developed. This is followed in Exercise 17 with an intensive motivic treatment in three parts below an unadorned melody.

The section ends with practice of canonic treatment. This may be considered difficult at this stage, but the intellectual effort involved is well worth while, both for this specific exercise and for the added command it gives of contrapuntal improvisation generally.

Exercise 13

Add a part below a chosen melody on these lines, using contrapuntal motivic treatment:

Old 100th

Organ

Exercise 14

Add a part above a melody, using left hand and pedals.
Note the imitation by diminution and inversion at the
opening.

Dundee

Exercise 15

Add two parts above a melody:

York

Organ

Exercise 16

Coloratura treatment. Here the tune is ornamented and elaborated into an expressive melodic line, with a simple three-part accompaniment on a second manual.

Schmücke Dich

Exercise 17

Add three parts below a melody, using consistent development of a short motive

(♪ ♩♩♩ ♩ etc.)

on the basis of similar examples in Bach's *Orgelbüchlein*:

Ravenshaw

Exercise 18

Canonic treatment. Study Bach's canonic preludes in his *Orgelbüchlein*. Do not hesitate to alter intervals and note values in the consequent, in the interest of a more convincing harmonic and contrapuntal result.

Organ

Nun komm der Heiden Heiland

Free Improvisation in Two Parts

Not only must each part have its own independent interest and vitality, but the parts in combination must create a purposeful scheme of harmonic progression and overall structure. For the first time in this course there is no pre-existent melody to hold the piece together. So the student

206

has to face the problem of the form. The most important elements are:

A coherent and shapely use of a limited amount of thematic material; and

A logical and well-balanced key scheme.

While the ultimate interest and value of a piece lies mainly in the invention and resourceful use of interesting material, the student's first need is the ability to plan a simple key structure with well-timed cadences and modulations, together with a fluency in the use of sequences.

Exercises 19–21 are concerned with short binary-form movements – short enough for the student to be able to memorize each half for a convincing repeat. It is important to think always in phrases and movement towards fresh key centres and cadences. If the given sketches are thoroughly practised, together with some prepared by the student, a sense of formal control should soon be acquired.

A point to watch here is that, when working without any notated sketch, students nearly always tend to move towards the subdominant early in the movement. This tendency should be resisted and movement towards nearly related keys on the sharp side cultivated instead. Too much stress on the subdominant side will always throw the tonal balance awry, and make a convincing return to the tonic key at the end of a piece more difficult to establish.

Exercise 19

Complete this binary-form sketch in the style of a minuet:

Organ

Sequence in G

(half close in C)

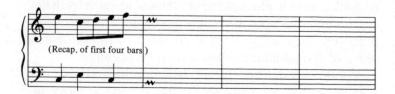

(Recap. of first four bars)

Exercise 20
Complete this binary-form sketch in the style of a march:

Reed
8′

Prin.
8′ 4′

208

(sequence)

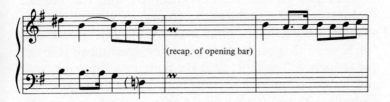

(to E minor)

(recap. of opening bar)

Exercise 21

Sketch on paper, and then complete at the keyboard, movements on similar lines, using these openings and later inventing your own:

(a)

209

Organ

(b)

(c)

(to B♭ major at
double bar)

Exercises 22 and 23 are concerned with the English voluntary of the eighteenth century. A careful analysis should be made of voluntaries by Stanley, Boyce and Greene, with special reference to key structure and the use of sequence. The most typical voluntary scheme is that of an introduction and allegro, both in the same key, but usually with a differing time signature. Both movements are based on the expansion of one thematic idea, the contrast being that of a broad and lyrical Diapason movement with a martial Trumpet or sparkling Cornet allegro.

Exercise 22

(a) Complete the following sketch, using a simple three-part texture:

Diapasons

210

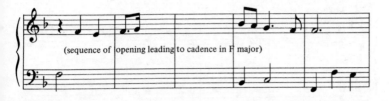

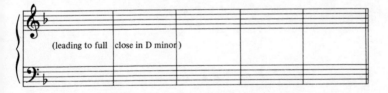

Sketch on paper and complete at the keyboard similar movements, using these openings and then inventing your own:

(b)

(modulation to G major)

Exercise 23

Complete the following sketch. Note the economy of material and the use of repetition and sequence.

Trumpet tune

Allegro

(sequence)

Short Contrapuntal Structures

Some effective models for short contrapuntal movements can be found in the organ masses and suites by French eighteenth-century composers. In particular, the following should be studied and analysed:

Couperin: *Messe pour les Paroisses* (L'Oiseau-Lyre edition)
Récit de Chromhorne (p. 14)
Dialogue (p. 24)
Tierce en Taille (p. 29)
Benedictus (p. 52)

Couperin: *Messe pour les Convents* (L'Oiseau-Lyre edition)
Récit de Chromhorne (p. 64)
Dialogue (p. 68)
Chromhorne sur la Taille (p. 78)
Elévation (p. 98)

Marchand: *Pièces d'orgue* (Schott edition)
Tierce en Taille (p. 26)
Tierce en Taille (p. 34)
Cromorne en Taille (p. 88)

de Grigny: *Messe* (Schola Cantorum edition)
Récit de Tierce en Taille (p. 19)
Récit de Tierce pour le Benedictus (p. 44)

de Grigny: *Hymnes* (Schola Cantorum edition)
Récit de Cromorne (p. 61)
Récit du Chant (p. 72)
Récit en Dialogue (p. 78)

Those slow movements which use the Cromorne or Tierce in the tenor register are very effective when used as Communion pieces, and no less so if this form inspires an improvisation along the same lines. This type of movement has an obvious affinity with slow chorale preludes of the German school in texture and meditative feeling. As with so much baroque music, it is essentially concerned with the expansion of one melodic idea. Here are two schemes for practice:

Exercise 24
Forty-eight bars, 4/4 time (Cromorne or Tierce en Taille idiom)
Eight bars introduction in imitative (three-part) style, tonic
Solo enters for four bars, tonic
Two bars rest for solo, tonic
Eight bars of solo, expanding to modulate to relative major or minor
Solo continues for six bars, leading back to tonic key; imperfect cadence
Solo rests for two bars
Solo enters with further expansion of material, modulating to dominant or relative major
Solo continues to the end in tonic

Exercise 25
Fifty bars, 4/4 time (dialogue or duo movement)
Twelve bars opening in imitative style, tonic
Eight bars modulating to supertonic minor
Six bars modulating to dominant
Eight bars modulating to tonic; imperfect cadence
Four bars modulating to subdominant
Twelve bars modulating back to tonic

Exercise 26
Complete this Tierce en Taille movement, based on the *Agnus Dei* from Merbecke's Communion Service:

Organ

Organ

Exercise 27

Improvise a Récit de Tierce based on the hymn 'Ad cenam Agni providi', beginning as follows:

Exercise 28

Improvise a Dialogue for Trumpet 8′ and Flutes 8′, 4′ and 2′ on the hymn 'A solis ortus cardine', beginning as follows:

218

(Trumpet)

Exercise 29

Improvise a Cromorne sur le Taille based on the hymn 'Adoro te devote', beginning as follows:

Organ

Exercise 30

Improvise a Récit de Cornet based on the hymn 'O Lux beata Trinitas', beginning as follows:

(Mode VIII)

Twenty-three
Organ Improvisation II

Binary, Ternary and Rondo Forms

These three forms are useful on many occasions – more especially for short introductory or closing voluntaries, and for examination purposes, where a more extended structure would be too long for the available time.

Binary Form
Revise 'Free Improvisation in Two Parts', pp. 206–13.

The minuet, with or without trio, is the most important form to analyse here. The most usual structure is as follows:

Sixteen bars modulating to the dominant or relative major key. (The first section may end in the tonic but I recommend a modulation.)

Eight bars leading back to the tonic for a restatement of the opening material. The last phrase is modified and extended by four bars. (Cf. Mozart: Symphony No. 39.) The trio follows a similar plan, but the first section usually closes in the tonic key.

As before, many movements on these lines should be sketched on paper, modelled on movements by Haydn and Mozart. When the basic plan has been memorized, improvized movements may be attempted. It is important for the student to analyse many eighteenth-century movements, with especial regard to harmonic rhythm.

Most students begin their training, both on paper and at the keyboard, with the chorale idiom, in which the har-

Organ

mony usually changes on each pulse of the bar. In a fast movement of the classical period the same harmony may be used for two or more bars, the interest being supplied by harmonic and melodic decoration. The student should attempt to improvise movements using the simplest harmonic basis, concentrating on the decoration (mainly in the melodic line) of this harmony, always trying to think in phrases.

Exercise 1
Complete this sketch at the keyboard:

(recap. of opening)

IIb IC V

Exercise 2
Elaborate this harmonic sketch, beginning as follows:

223

Organ

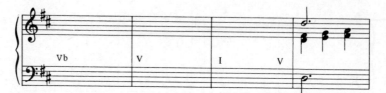

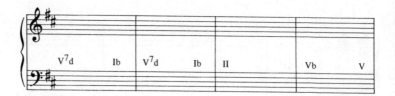

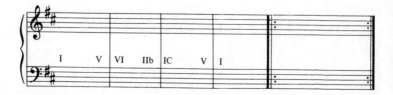

Improvise a second half on the same lines as Exercise 1.

The student should now make his own sketches for elaboration, using either his own harmonic basis, or one derived from movements by Haydn or Mozart.

Ternary Form

The minuet with trio, and then repeated, is of course an example of ternary form in its overall shape. An effective form for short slow movements is the closed ternary form, where the first section closes in the tonic key. There is a middle section on new material in a related key, and the form is completed with a restatement of the opening, perhaps shortened and varied, followed by a coda. The Intermezzo in E flat, Op. 117, by Brahms is a useful model for this kind of structure. Once again, sketch out movements on paper, and then elaborate at the keyboard.

224

Exercise 3
Complete and elaborate the following:

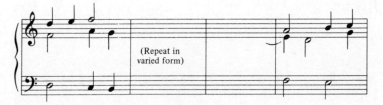

(Repeat in varied form)

(End of first section

link

Organ

poco animato

(into G minor for | contrasting middle | section) (develop with

(some use of sequence | to a climax)

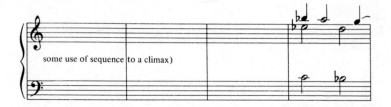

Rall.

(leading to recap. of | opening)

(Repeat eight bars of opening and add six bars of coda.)

Rondo Form

The simplest and most useful structure to practise is to be found in the chaconnes of Louis Couperin. In his C major Chaconne an eight-bar theme is repeated between episodes of the same length, the whole piece having a stately, sarabande-like dance character. A more developed treatment could use a sixteen-bar section in binary form as the rondo theme, with three episodes of the same length. The keys used in the episodes might be:

Tonic major or minor;
Relative major or minor;
Subdominant major or minor.

226

Exercise 4

Complete and elaborate the following:

(a) Refrain

I (in F)   V   IIb V   I

(in D minor)

(b)

Ib   IV   IVb

V   I

(c)

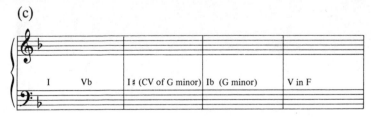

I   Vb   I♯ (CV of G minor)   Ib (G minor)   V in F

Organ

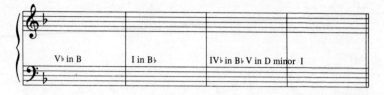

Vb in B   I in Bb   IVb in Bb V in D minor I

(d)

(♩   ♪)

(in C)

(♩   ♪)

V in A minor Ib   IV⁷   V   I

(e)

I in A minor IIb   V   Vb   I   V   I

(in D minor) (in C)

Vb   I   VI   VIIb   V   I(♮)

(D minor)

228

Fugue and Fugato, including Chorale Treatments

The student must achieve competence and fluency on paper before beginning this section. It is important that a good textbook should be used, but it is even more desirable that the student should analyse organ fugues by Buxtehude, Bach and their predecessors, and model his own work on them.

When a reasonable facility has been acquired on paper, the student should begin at the keyboard with the improvisation of answers to the given subjects. The subjects should be treated at different octave pitches, including the use of the pedal. When this can be done readily, the next step is to practise the improvisation of counter-subjects to the subjects and the answers. This should not prove unduly difficult, with the technique acquired as a result of the work on previous sections. A complete exposition in three parts should then be attempted, rounding off with a short coda. This fughetta form is not too difficult to organize, and is an effective way of rounding off a hymn, or providing a short interlude in the course of the liturgy.

The exercises below are concerned with longer fugal structures, including two middle entries in related keys, and linking episodic material. All this work may be linked with 'Free Improvisation in Two Parts' (pp. 206–13) by the analysis of the fugal movements in the voluntaries of Stanley and Boyce. Similarly, the work on fugue may be linked with 'Chorale and Hymn Tune Treatments' (pp. 200–6) with the study of the fugal treatment of chorales, in which each line of the melody is anticipated by a fugal treatment of a subject derived from it by diminution and variation.

Fugal improvisation is one of the most interesting and impressive techniques in this art, and its study at this point is to be seen as a logical outcome of the work previously done.

Organ

Exercise 5

Improvise answers to the following subjects:

(a) Stanley

(b) du Mage

(c) Boyce

(d) Buxtehude

Exercise 6

Using the subjects from Exercise 5, the student should now improvise counter-subjects above and below, repeating the procedure with the improvised answers. When this work is fluent, a complete exposition may be attempted, together with a short coda to make a brief fughetta in three voices.

Exercise 7

Complete this sketch at the keyboard:

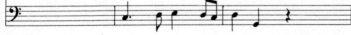

Organ

Exercise 8
Complete this sketch at the keyboard:

Exercise 9

Sketch on paper and complete at the keyboard fughettas on similar lines to the preceding exercises, using the following subjects:

(a)

(b)

(c)

Ground Bass and Variations

There are many splendid examples of the ground bass, passacaglia or chaconne in the literature of the organ: for instance those by Buxtehude (D minor, E minor and C minor), Bach (C minor), Rheinberger (E minor, Sonata No. 8) and Reger (D minor and F minor).

Most basses will permit at least six different harmonizations, and further variety may be obtained with the use of chromaticism and accented passing notes. The essence of a successful treatment is the appropriate juxtaposition of harmonizations, producing a cumulative build up of interest and tension, together with interesting motivic and decorative elaborations of the basic harmony.

A third important point is in the dove-tailing of variants so that the flow is maintained, and a feeling of squareness of phrasing avoided. This may be achieved by overlapping each motivic treatment with the bass. My complete working of (d) below shows how this may be done.

When fluency has been gained, then a start should be made on working these harmonic variants into a contrapuntal texture by means of motivic imitation. The number of possible rhythmic figures is by no means limitless and it should not take long to learn at least twelve treatments. (See examples.) These should be practised until facility is acquired.

The last stage is the improvisation of a short introduction and a coda, which should make some reference to the introduction. The material should be derived from the bass, and be treated in rhetorical and rhapsodic manner to act as a foil to the strictness of the recurrent bass pattern.

The ability to create variations is fundamental to both composition and improvisation, since the form is concerned with the extraction of the maximum possibilities from a small amount of thematic material. The first type to be practised is the melodic and contrapuntal decoration of the basic harmonic skeleton of the theme. The best works for study are three sets of variations by Brahms: the two books on a theme by Paganini, the Handel set, and the 'St Anthony Chorale' Variations. Dupré's *Variations sur un Noël* are also well worth the most careful study.

The chosen theme should first be analysed thoroughly for its varied harmonic possibilities, and any canonic treatments that suggest themselves. As with ground-bass work, there are a number of motivic formulae that may be adapted to suit the treatment suggested by the character of the theme. The order of variants needs careful thought to ensure variety and an overall sense of progression. An extended fugal treatment and closing toccata is an effective method of concluding a set of variations. My *Variations on 'Amazing Grace'* (Novello) were composed to illustrate this chapter.

Ground Bass Treatments

Organ

Exercise 10
Analyse the following basses on the same lines:

(a)

(b)

(c)

Exercise 11
Elaborate the harmonies used in the above basses on the lines of these variants which I suggest for (c):

(1)

(2)

(3)

(4)

(5)

(6)

(7)

(8)

Organ

(9)

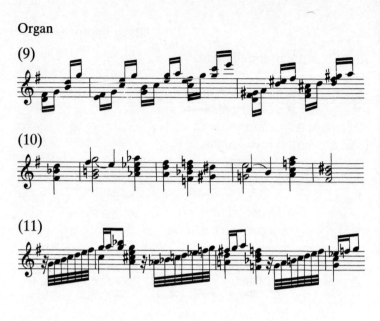

(10)

(11)

(12)

Sonata Structures

The first point to be grasped here is that sonata form as derived from the classics is primarily concerned with the balance and manipulation of tonality, rather than with thematic contrast or development, though these elements often play an important part in such movements. Many sonata movements, both early and mature, and including those of Haydn and Mozart, were mono-thematic, and it is suggested that the student's first attempts should be along these lines. To this end the following movements should be carefully analysed, and movements based on these plans should be sketched on paper, using the student's own thematic material and rhythmic patterns:

Haydn: Symphonies Nos. 88, 100, 103 and 104

Mozart: Symphony No. 35 and the finale of Symphony No. 39

The second point concerns the relationship between sonata

form and the rounded binary form, which has been studied here in the context of the minuet and trio. Sonata form is best thought of as an extension of this smaller structure. Preserving the binary idea, the first section is extended to include a transition to the dominant or relative major for either a varied restatement of the opening theme, or some fresh material (second subject). We close in the new key at the double bar with a short coda, and this completes the exposition.

The second part of the binary scheme begins with a modulating section which will use motives from the exposition, or introduce new material of an episodic character. This so-called 'development' section need not necessarily be based on the main thematic material; it is often as effective to use motives from the transitional or codetta sections. This development section is misnamed because its main function is to modulate and expand the two tonalities of the exposition. The fact that it thereby uses material from the exposition is incidental, but this procedure does help to ensure coherence and unity.

This modulating section, which may be quite short, then leads back to the tonic key for the recapitulation. Here the tonic key is maintained, apart from brief episodes of tonal colour. The recapitulation should balance the exposition in length, and may include a fairly extended coda. All the material of the exposition may be restated in the recapitulation, but obviously the second subject will be transposed into the tonic key. This will necessarily entail modification of the transitional material. One of the most fascinating aspects of analysis is to note how the great classical composers have dealt with this problem.

My own *Toccata* (published by Novello, together with the *Variations on 'Amazing Grace'*) is based closely on the structural plan of the first movement of Mozart's Symphony No. 40 in G minor. It demonstrates how a movement using twentieth-century materials may be constructed on classical formal schemes. It should be carefully compared with the Mozart model.

Organ

Exercise 12

Improvise the exposition of a movement in sonata form based on the subjects given below. A preliminary sketch on paper should be made. The material for the subjects is taken from the hymn 'Aeternae Rex altissime'.

(a)

(b)

Exercise 13

Extend the exposition into a development section, recapitulation and coda, with a preliminary sketch on paper.

Once some facility has been acquired on a fairly large time scale, the student may attempt a work in three or four movements. Some material based on the plainchant hymn above is given for such practice.

Exercise 14
Improvise a slow movement in ternary form, based on the
following opening:

Exercise 15
Improvise a scherzo in rondo form, based on the following
opening:

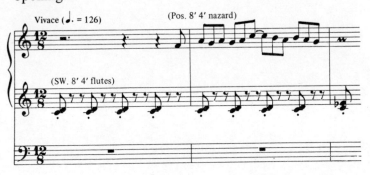

Exercise 16
Improvise a finale, consisting of introduction, fugue and
toccata, based on this fugue subject:

241

Organ

It will be noticed that this scheme of study in organ improvisation follows fairly closely the historical evolution of organ music as discussed in the earlier part of this book. A mastery of classical technique is certainly the best basis for further development along more contemporary lines, but it is true to say that further progress will be limited only by the student's innate powers of invention and imagination.

Postscript
Deus ex Machina

'In the beginning was the Word ... And the Word was made Flesh. ...' How the organist is to make the Word manifest from the 'wondrous machine' to the listener has been the theme of this book. The Word to be made sound and significance may vary from a secular estampie to the rich symbolism of Messiaen's *Les Corps glorieux*.

It is precisely its mechanical nature, providing the distancing of the player from the instrument, and the listeners from both, that makes the organ the supreme God-instrument. The most obvious disadvantage of the instrument is seen to be its noblest feature, enabling it to speak in the calmest serenity – with a 'still small voice' or with the 'commanding sounds' to compose and charm. The immediacy of contact which all other instrumentalists possess – and the human voice itself above all others – speaks of the human; the organ of the divine. The storms of human passion and anguish are foreign to its nature. Organists have to work with the instruments they find to hand: whatever the machine, we still have to find the God in it. The crowd will talk through voluntaries, and the critics will continue to ignore it; but both will on occasion stand in awe at a sound that is beyond the transitory joys and sorrows of earthly life. Then it is that God and the wondrous machine are one, and will speak the Word.

Glossary

Anches: the French term for reed stops, considered as a chorus.

Backfall: that part of a mechanical action which transfers the upward movement at the distal end of the key to a downward movement pulling down the tracker.

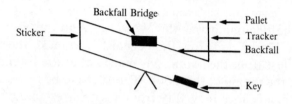

Basse de Tierce: a classical French registration, usually based on the *Grand Orgue*'s 16′ and 8′ pitches (Flutes). It is effectively a 16′ Cornet, i.e., 16.8.5⅓.4.3⅕. and sometimes including 2⅔′ and 2′. It is most often used for the bass line in duos and trios.

Bourdon: most usually the stopped pipes an octave below the main 8′ rank in French organs; in England it is the basic 16′ rank in the Pedal Organ.

Blockwerk: the undivided pitch structure of the medieval organ, i.e., the basic chorus sound, without the possibility of stopping off separate pitches.

Brustwerk: means 'in the breast' of the German organ, with its pipe chest encased below the *Hauptwerk* (or Great Organ). The early examples were usually Regals and retained this character when flue ranks were also present. This position below the main case was sometimes used by French builders for an internal *Positif* division.

Cantus firmus: a 'fixed melody', usually of plainchant or chorale origin, used as the basis of a piece in contrapuntal texture. It could be placed in any part or 'voice' and was often given to the pedals at 8′ or 4′ pitch.

Chair Organ: the English name for the 'organ behind the bench', i.e., the same as the German *Rückpositiv* or French *Positif*. The term Choir Organ is found as early as 1699 and the similarity of the names has led to some confusion.

Chorus: the grouping of stops, often in families, as in the *Blockwerk* or the French *plein jeu* (both mainly Principal tone), or the reeds and Cornets ensemble of the *grands jeu*.

Console: the playing apparatus at which the organist sits, often in a loft or tribune, consisting of one or more keyboards (manuals), pedals (sometimes) and the stop mechanism.

244

Cornet: a five- or six-rank combination: 8.4.(4).2⅔.2.1⅗. The pitches may all be present in one stop, as in the English Mounted Cornet, or that on the French *Récit* or *Grand Orgue*. Or it may be a stop comprising the two or three upper ranks such as the Sesquialtera. It may also be assembled from separate ranks, and was an essential element in the *grands jeu.*

Cremona: a rank often found in the Choir or Chair Organ in England from the end of the seventeenth century. It is usually a more suave equivalent of the French Cromorne and the German Krummhorn. In the nineteenth century it was usually supplanted by the Clarinet on the Solo Organ.

Coupler: a device that allows the pedal or manual keys to pull down the corresponding keys of another manual, or manuals. After the development of the instrument away from the single *Blockwerk* principal into several contrasting divisions: Chair; *Brustwerk*; Echo, etc., it was a means for the re-unification of the tonal resources of all these divisions into tuttis of varying dynamic levels and colours.

Cut-up: a builder's term for the height of the mouth of a flue pipe considered as a fraction of its width, 1 in 4 for instance. The smaller the cut-up the more lively the sound.

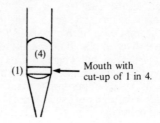

Mouth with cut-up of 1 in 4.

Double-draw stops have two positions, half and full, which allow two ranks, perhaps of short compass, to be controlled by one stop knob.

Echo box: a precursor of the Swell Organ in that shutters were applied to the totally enclosed Echo division in England and later to the *Récit* in France. Hence the wide dynamic range these manuals eventually acquired.

Fiffaro: a rank found in Italian instruments of the late Renaissance period, sometimes as a treble half-stop. It is an undulating (tuned sharp) rank to be used with the *Principale* in such expressive pieces as the toccatas 'per elevatione' of Frescobaldi.

Flue: the windway in an organ pipe from the foothole to the mouth, where the air is directed on to the upper lip. 'Flues' or 'flue stops' are distinct from 'reeds' or 'reed stops' in which the sound is produced by means of a beating reed.

Flute: a stop of metal or wood, obviously imitative, designed to offer a more gentle contrast to the Principal chorus and originating from its use in Portative, Positive and Chamber Organs.

Organ

Fonds: the French term for foundation stops, i.e., Principals and Flutes of (16'), 8' and 4' pitch.

Fourniture: the basic French mixture which 'furnishes' the full chorus based on foundation stops of 8' pitch.

Grands jeu: the reed chorus of the classical (seventeenth- and eighteenth-century) French organ (*Grand Orgue + Positif*), reinforced by Cornets, Tierces and Prestants 4'.

Great Organ: the main keyboard of the English organ corresponding to the *Grande Orgue* in France and the *Hauptwerk* in Germany.

Jeu doux: a French term for a soft foundation chorus, usually of Flute tone, at (16'), 8' and 4' pitch.

Key: the lever that the player moves with his fingers in order to activate the mechanism that admits air into the pipe.

Manual ('hand'), the name given to a keyboard as opposed to a pedal board.

Montre: the Principal rank of a French organ and may be of 32', 16' or 8' pitch. A Prestant is a Montre of 4' pitch.

Mécanique suspendu: an action, developed mainly in France, whereby the sticker pulls down the key directly without backfall. Its advantage is in the immediacy and lightness of touch thus provided.

Mutation stops are those that change the name of the note being played, e.g. Nazards and Tierces.

Oberwerk might be the name given to the main division of the organ (as appears to be implied in Bach's *'Dorian' Toccata*) or it can mean a more lightly scaled division placed on a chest above the *Hauptwerk*.

Organo pleno means 'full organ' but its use in German eighteenth-century music appears to imply the use of a substantial chorus on one or more manuals as seems appropriate to the character of the piece, i.e., it might include a basic mixture such as the Fourniture, but not necessarily 16', Cymbal or reeds.

Organum: the medieval practice of singing in parallel fifths and octaves, from which independent polyphony eventually evolved. Any connection of the term with organ is conjectural.

Pallet: the valve below the pipe chest that controls the admission of air into the foot of the pipe. Precision and sensitivity in the control of this action is the prime purpose of both builder and player. The first aim may be achieved by non-mechanical systems; the second only by finely engineered tracker actions.

Plein jeu: the French term for the full Principal chorus from 16' to Cymbale on *Grand orgue* and *Positif*.

Portative: a small, easily moved organ, which might be placed on a table or carried in a procession.

Positive: a small organ that could be placed where needed in any part of a large church, or used domestically. Its eventual amalgamation with the *Blockwerk* either internally or as a Chair Organ (*Rückpositiv*) was one of the most significant developments in the evolution of the organ, making available many possibilities of textural contrast, such as solo and accompaniment.

Principal: the open metal pipes of the *Blockwerk* from 16' to Cymbal. It is often used specifically of those ranks of 16′, 8′ and 4′ pitch.

Pulldown: a pedal key that has no separate pipe to sound but merely pulls down the required manual key to provide a sustained note or 'point', thereby leaving both hands free for figurative textures above it. Short pedal boards of this kind were introduced into some Italian Renaissance organs.

Rank: an assembly of pipes of one timbre, such as Principal, Flute or Trumpet. It can be of full or short compass, as in the classical French organ.

Récit originated in the French classical organ as a short compass solo manual, usually placed above and behind the *Grand Orgue* and containing a Cornet and possibly a Trumpet. In the nineteenth century it evolved into the shuttered-box 'expressive' manual of the Cavaillé-Coll organ and was given a full range of soft foundation, undulating and powerful reed stops.

Reed: that part of a reed-pipe that holds the brass tongue that vibrates in the wind held within the boot of the pipe.

Regal: a late fifteenth-century small keyboard instrument in which the sound is produced by a set of beating reeds with small resonators. It was eventually incorporated into the organ, placed usually either in the *Brustwerk* or the *Positiv*.

Registration: the art of choosing stops appropriate to the music being interpreted and therefore largely dependent on the performer's knowledge of historical styles of organ-building and composition. It is necessarily limited by the resources of any given instrument.

Scale: the comparative sizes, in particular the diameter, of pipes; often described as being 'narrow' or 'wide' scaled.

Sesquialtera: a mutation stop which at different periods has contained a Twelfth and Tierce, or more ranks, giving it a mixture character. Depending on its structure, it can be used in Cornet-like solo combinations, or as a chorus stop bridging the gap between flue and reed choruses.

Slider: either an early key mechanism in which a hole would be pushed under the pipe to govern the admittance of wind *or* a perforated strip of wood that controls the admittance of wind to a complete rank of pipes. It is activated by a stop mechanism that enables the player to choose between and separate the ranks of a *Blockwerk*.

Split keys are found in mean-tuned instruments to allow, for example, D sharp and E flat to sound separate pitches.

Stop: a device for shutting off those ranks of pipes not required by the organist.

Swell: a division enclosed in a box and shuttered, thus allowing dynamic variation. First developed in Spain and England it has been applied to several manuals including the Choir, Solo and *Brustwerk* and even (logically) to the whole organ in the interests of dynamic variety and 'expression'. This trend has been abandoned with the current re-assessment of the true nature of the instrument.

Tirasses: the French term for the manual to pedal coupler.

Tracker: that part of a mechanical action that conveys the movement of the finger on the key to the pallet by pulling it down. *See* **Backfall**.

Trio: an idiomatic organ texture in which the upper parts are either played on the same or separate manuals while the bass part is played on another manual or the pedals. Both types were cultivated by the classical French school of composers but the most fully developed works in the idiom were written by J. S. Bach.

Tremblant 'fort' or 'doux' is the French term for Tremulant. This device, usually affecting the whole organ, was common as early as the sixteenth century. It is generally undervalued today, probably as a persistent reaction against its ubiquity in the 'entertainment' organ of the cinema and the home.

Ventil: a system, much developed by Cavaillé-Coll, in which the 'families' of stops on any division were placed on separate chests controlled by a ventil or valve which was operated by a pedal. The reed choruses on *Positif*, *Grand Orgue* and *Pédale* could be 'prepared' and brought on as required. Vierne's scores clearly demonstrate this practice.

Verset: a French term denoting a piece of organ music that is designed to alternate with verses of plainchant in a performance of such liturgical pieces as the Mass, Magnificat or Office Hymn.

Voluntary: an English term for an organ piece that does not have such an obligatory connection with the liturgy as the verse or verset.

Wind chest: the box that stores the wind on which the ranks of pipes are mounted. Air is admitted into the foot of the pipe by a pallet activated by a mechanism and controlled by a keyboard. Ranks may be stopped off or brought on by a slider or spring device.

Music:
Recommended Editions

The editions listed below are the best and most useful known to the author, but research is constantly revealing fresh sources that must necessarily lead to revision of such editions.

Apel, Willi, (ed.), *Keyboard Music of the Fourteenth and Fifteenth Centuries*, (American Institute of Musicology, 1963)

Bach, Johann Sebastian, New Bärenreiter Edition, (Peters, 1969)

Blow, John, *Complete Organ Works*, Watkins Shaw (ed.), (Schott, 1972, No. 10595)

Boyce, William, *Ten Voluntaries*, facsimile edition, (OUP, 1972)

Brahms, Johannes, *Eleven Chorale Preludes*, John E. West (ed.), (Novello, 1928, or Peters, 1964)

Buxheimer Orgelbuch, 2 vols., Alan Booth (ed.), (Hinrichsen, 1959)

Buxtehude, Dietrich, *Sämtliche Orgelwerke*, 4 vols., Hedar (ed.), (Hansen, 1952)

Cabezón, Antonio de, *Tientos et Fugues*, Kastner (ed.), (Schott, No. 4948)

Cabezón, Antonio de, Selection, Straube (ed.), (Alto Meisler, 1925)

Cavazzoni, Girolamo, *Orgelwerke*, 2 vols., Mischiati (ed.), (Schott Nos. 4991 and 4992)

Couperin, François, *Two Organ Masses*,[1] P. Brunold (ed.), revised edition, 1982

Franck, César, *Organ Works*, (Durand, 1936)[2]

Frescobaldi, Girolamo, *Orgel und Klavierwerke*, 5 vols., Pidoux (ed.), (Bärenreiter, 1959)

Gabrieli, Andrea, *Orgelwerke*, 5 vols., Pidoux (ed.), (Bärenreiter, 1953)

Handel, George Frideric, *Concertos*, Chrysander (ed.), German Handel Society or Kalmus

Handel, George Frideric, *Six Concertos for the Harpsichord or Organ* (Walsh's Transcriptions, 1738), William D. Gudger (ed.), (A–R Editions, Madison, Wisconsin, USA, 1981)

Haydn, Franz Joseph, *32 Pieces*, A. Nagel (ed.), (Hanover, 1931)

Liszt, Franz, *Organ Works*, 4 vols., Margittay (ed.), (Boosey & Hawkes, 1971)

Organ

Locke, Matthew, *Organ Voluntaries*, Thurston Dart (ed.), (Stainer and Bell, 1957)

Mendelssohn, Felix, *Organ Works*, (Peters, No. 852, or Novello)

Mozart, Wolfgang Amadeus, *Andante in F* (K.616)[3]

Mozart, Wolfgang Amadeus, *Fantasia in F minor* (K.594), Wills (ed.), (OUP)

Mozart, Wolfgang Amadeus, *Fantasia in F minor* (K.608)[4]

Mulliner Book, Stevens (ed.), (Stainer and Bell, 1973)

Mussorgsky, Modest, *Pictures at an Exhibition*, Wills (trans.), (Oecumuse, 1983)

Nares, James, *Six Fugues with Introductory Voluntaries*, facsimile edition, (OUP, 1974)

Purcell, Henry, *Complete Organ Works*, H. McLean (ed.), (Novello, 1957)

Scheidt, Samuel, *Ausgewahlte Werke*, Keller (ed.), (Peters, 1968)

Schumann, Robert, *Organ Works*, (Augener, 1925, Nos. 6428 and 6429, or Novello, OUP or Peters)

Stanley, John, *Thirty Voluntaries*, facsimile edition, (OUP, 1957)

Sweelinck, Jan, *Keyboard Works*, Seiffert (ed.), (Hinrichsen, 1943)

Titelouze, Jean, *Oeuvres complètes d'orgue*, Guilmant (ed.), (Schott, 1967)

Wesley, Samuel, *Twelve Voluntaries*, Op. 6, Francis Routh (ed.), (Concordia, USA, 1983)

---

[1] Other composers of the French classical school are available either through Éditions Musicales de la Schola Cantorum, N. Dufourcq (ed.), or through Schott, A. Guilmant (ed.).

[2] Use the original Durand edition, but there are errors, even in the recent revision. Consult the Dupré edition (Bornemann) for ideas that he claims reveal Franck's intentions more closely.

[3] This is best played from the original three-stave layout in the complete edition.

[4] Novello, Peters and Bornemann publish versions of this piece. I recommend that the student does his own transcription, consulting Mozart's own piano-duet versions and any of the others to find a suitable solution.

Recommended Recordings

This list will necessarily be of ephemeral usefulness as even the finest of recordings has a limited availability. Re-issues and second-hand copies are well worth looking out for. The list has been selected with relevance to specific points made in the text.

Whatever its value and importance, it is a mistake to regard any performance as having definitive status. It should be possible to learn from almost any performance, but it is an error to use one as a model or touchstone.

J. S. Bach: Complete Works   Marie-Claire Alain, Peter Hurford or Helmut Walcha
A critical comparison of these performances will provide a comprehensive basis for the student's exploration into Bach interpretation.

Bach, transcribed Wills: Nine Movements   Arthur Wills Hyperion A66119

Blow: Echo Voluntary in G *and* Voluntary in A   Arthur Wills E77013

Buxtehude: Complete Works   Lionel Rogg   IC 137 16351–8

Brahms: Complete Works   Peter Planyavsky   2740 276

Cabezón: Selected Pieces   Francis Chapelet   HM 765

Cochereau, Pierre, Improvisations at Notre Dame   Phillips 641732LL

Couperin: The Two Masses   Ton Koopman   6768 346

Dupré: Selected Pieces   Jean Guillou   FC506

Elgar: Sonata in G, Op. 28   Simon Preston   2RG 528

English Choral Works   Choir of Ely Cathedral, organ accompaniment: Stephen le Prevost   A66012

Franck: Complete Works   Marie-Claire Alain   STU 71035–7

Frescobaldi: Selected Pieces   Lionel Rogg   2C069 73038

Handel: Organ Concertos, Nos. 1–15   Simon Preston and the Menuhin Festival Orchestra   SLS 624

Hindemith: Three Sonatas   Lionel Rogg   MUS 23

Howells: Selected Pieces   Michael Nicholas   VPSO 101

Ligeti: *Volumina and* Etude No. 1   Gerd Zacher   HR2543 618

Liszt: Selected Important Works   Ernst-Erich Stender   M 1055

Mendelssohn: Complete Works   Hans Fagius   B1SLP 156–7

Organ

Messiaen: The composer's own recordings, though long deleted from British catalogues, are the important ones to hear. Jennifer Bate's complete recording project has won high praise from the composer and from critics.

Mozart: Epistle Sonatas for Organ and Orchestra Christopher Hogwood and the Academy of Ancient Music D28602

Mozart: Pieces for Mechanical Organ Lionel Rogg SLS 6218

Mussorgsky, transcribed Wills: *Pictures at an Exhibition* Arthur Wills Hyperion AS66006

Poulenc: Organ Concerto in G minor Maurice Duruflé and the French National Radio Orchestra, conducted by Georges Prêtre ASD 2835

Purcell: Voluntary for a Double Organ Arthur Wills E77013

Reubke: *Sonata on the 94th Psalm* John Scott ACA 507

Saint-Saëns: Symphony No. 3 Gaston Litaize and the Chicago Symphony Orchestra, conducted by Daniel Barenboim 3300619

Schoenberg: Variations on a Recitative, Op. 40 Ivor Bolton WS195

Sweelinck: Selected Pieces Francis Chapelet HM 948

Vierne: The Six Symphonies Pierre Cochereau FYO28–32

Widor: Symphonies I and IV Arthur Wills RL25033

Wills: Symphonic Suite: *The Fenlands* Arthur Wills and the Cambridge Band Hyperion A66068

Wills, Arthur, *Variations on 'Amazing Grace'* Meridian E77014.

Bibliography

Suggestions for Further Reading

The historical studies by William Sumner and Peter Williams will make the most useful starting point. These should be followed by such nationally based studies as Clutton and Niland's *The British Organ* and Fenner Douglas's *The Language of the Classical French Organ*.

The importance of keeping in touch with fresh thinking about the instrument through reputable periodicals was mentioned in my *Foreword*. The stimulus thus provided will surely lead the student along ever widening paths of discovery and interest.

Arnold, C. R., *Organ Literature*, (Scarecrow Press, 1973)

Bach, Carl Philipp Emanuel, *Essay on the True Art of Playing Keyboard Instruments*, (Eulenberg, 1974)

Bédos de Celles, Dom Francis, *L'Art du facteur d'orgues*, C. Ferguson (trans.), (Sunbury Press, Raleigh, North Carolina, USA, 1977)

Brown, Howard Mayer, *Embellishing Sixteenth-Century Music*, (OUP, 1976)

Brown, T., 'Schumann's Baroque Organ Compositions', *Diapason*, April 1977

Bukofzer, M. F., *Music in the Baroque Era*, (Norton, 1947)

Burney, Charles, *The Present State of Music in Germany, the Netherlands and the United Provinces* (1773), Percy Scholes (ed.), (London, 1959)

Butler, D. L., 'The Organ Works of Mendelssohn', 3 parts, *Diapason*, February 1978, April 1978, June 1978

Clark, J. B., 'American Organ Music before 1830', *Diapason*, November 1981

Clutton, C., and A. Niland, *The British Organ*, (Batsford, 1963; revised, 1982)

Cole, Hugo, *Sounds and Sense: Aspects of Musical Notation*, (OUP, 1974)

Colles, H. C., *Walford Davies*, (OUP, 1942)

Couperin, François, *L'Art de toucher le clavecin*, A. Linde (ed.), (Breitkopf & Härtel, 1961)

Dart, Thurston, *The Interpretation of Music*, (Hutchinson's University Library, 1954)

Douglas, Fenner, *The Language of the Classical French Organ*, (Yale University Press, 1969)

Edskes, B. H., *Arp Schnitger en zijn Werk in Het Groningerland*, (Groningen, 1969)

Emery, Walter, *Bach's Ornaments*, (Novello, 1957)

Eschbach, J. E., 'The Cavaillé-Coll Grand Orgue in St Sulpice', *Diapason*, September 1976

Ferguson, Howard, *Keyboard Interpretation*, (OUP, 1975)

Organ

Franck, César, *V. d'Indy*, R. Newmarch (trans), (London, 1922)

Hass, R., 'Ars Organica Danica',[1] *Diapson*, January 1979

Henrich-Schneider, Eta, *The Harpsichord*, (Concordia, 1954)

Holden, D. J., 'The Tonal Evolution of the E. M. Skinner Organ', 5 parts, *Diapason*, July 1977, February 1978, June 1978, March 1979, January 1980

Hopkins, E. J., and E. F. Rimbault, *The Organ*, (London, 1877)

Hradetzky, G., 'Organ-Building in Austria', *ISO Information*, 10 (1973)

Kratzenstein, M., 'A Survey of Organ Literature and Editions: Scandinavia', *Diapason*, April 1976

Lang, P. J., *Music in Western Civilisation*, (Dent, 1942)

Lowery, H., *The Background of Music*, (Hutchinson's University Library, 1952)

McKinnon, J., 'The Tenth-Century Organ at Winchester', *Organ Year Book*, Vol. 5 (1974)

Messiaen, Olivier, *The Technique of my Musical Language*, (Leduc, 1956)

Murray, T., 'A Performance Style for Mendelssohn', *Diapason*, August 1976

Organ Year Book, 5 (1974), 4–19

Parks, A., 'William Albright's *Organbook 1* – a Master Lesson', *Diapason*, May 1978

Peterson, J. D., 'Schumann's Fugues on BACH', *Diapason*, May 1982

Phelps, L., 'The Future of the Organ', *Diapason*, January 1980

Phelps, L., 'Introspection', *Diapason*, June 1979

Planyavsky, P., 'Retro-Suspection', *Diapason*, June 1979

Routh, Francis, *Early English Organ Music*, (Barrie & Jenkins, 1973)

Sadie, Stanley, *Handel Concertos*, (BBC Music Guides, 1972)

Schlick, Arnolt, *Spiegel der Organmacher und Organisten* (1511), (Frits Knuf Publishers, 1982)

Shostakovich, Dmitry, *Testimony* (Hamish Hamilton, 1979)

Searle, Humphrey, *The Music of Liszt*, (Dover Books, 1966)

Spark, W., *Musical Memories*, (London, 19?)

Stevens, Denis, *Musicology*, (Macdonald Futura, 1980)

Sumner, William, *The Organ*, (Macdonald, 3rd ed., 1962)

Vivian, A. L., 'G. Donald Harrison – A Study of Several Organ Designs', *Diapason*, January 1978

Weir, Gillian, 'The Organ – Medium or Message?', *Diapason*, February 1979

Williams, Peter, *Bach Organ Music*, (BBC Music Guides, 1972)

Williams, Peter, *The European Organ 1450–1850*, (Batsford, 1966)

Williams, Peter, *Figured Bass Accompaniment*, 2 vols., (Edinburgh Press, 1970)

Williams, Peter, *A New History of the Organ*, (Faber and Faber, 1980)

Williams, Peter, *The Organ Music of J. S. Bach*, 2 vols., (Cambridge University Press, 1980)

---

[1] This article comments on trends in Danish organ-building, with reference to Anderson organs, which are described as 'univeral organs for playing the entire organ literature'.

Select Index of Names

Organ

Praetorius, 21, 46
Purcell, 63, 78, 128, 135, 174

Radulescu, Michael, 149
Ravel, 106, 161, 169
Reger, 27, 95, 96–8, 105, 106, 120, 122, 124, 139, 148, 149, 153
Reubke, 94–5, 96
Rheinberger, Josef, 160–1
Roussel, 150

Saint-Saëns, 159–60
Scheidemann, Heinrich, 46
Scheidt, 46, 53, 54, 69, 126
Schnitger, Arp, 20, 48, 53, 64, 75, 133, 149
Schoenberg, 97, 124, 127, 139, 148, 149
Schumann, 21, 39, 89–90, 91, 95, 104, 139, 166
Schweitzer, Albert, 15, 19, 20, 29, 105, 127
Silbermann, Gottfried, 65, 66, 71, 75, 84, 133, 144
Slonimsky, Sergey, 151
Stainer, 175
Stanford, 121, 122, 174, 176
Stanley, John, 81, 128, 135

Strauss, 22, 96, 98, 121, 138, 159, 160
Sweelinck, 27, 46–7, 48, 51, 53, 73
Titelouze, 27, 44, 48, 55, 56, 68, 107
Tomkins, Thomas, 62
Tournemire, Charles, 106, 107, 108–9
Travers, John, 81
Vaughan Williams, 14, 122, 176
Vierne, 14, 16, 20, 29, 30–1, 39, 90, 94, 99, 101, 102, 107, 108, 113, 132, 135, 161
Vivaldi, 27, 80, 164, 166
Vogler, Georg Joseph, 166
Wagner, 90, 97, 111, 117, 121, 138, 166, 167
Walton, 160
Weelkes, 62
Werckmeister, Andreas, 64, 138
Wesley, Samuel, 115–16
Wesley, S. S., 116–17, 174, 175
Widor, 20, 90, 99, 101, 105–6, 107, 109, 113, 126, 160, 161
Williams, Peter, 51, 133
Willis, Henry, 118–19, 120, 121, 126
Wills, Arthur, 133, 152, 161, 162–3

Index of Organs Figures in **bold type** indicate specifications